THE HUMANITY OF GOD

It was Pope Pius XII who described KARL BARTH as 'the greatest theologian since St. Thomas Aquinas'. Certainly he has had an immense influence over the whole course of Protestant theology in our time, and is regarded with admiration and respect even by those who do not share his views. From the time of his *Commentary on Romans*, in 1919, when he was pastor in a small Swiss village, through the years of teaching in the universities of Göttingen, Münster and Bonn, and finally, after refusing to take the oath of loyalty to Hitler, back to his native Switzerland and the chair of theology in Basel, he has been an explosive figure in the realms of both theology and politics. For close on fifty years he has been in the forefront of the struggle to shape a theology that lets nothing of the great past of Christianity go, and yet speaks afresh to each situation in our time.

The three essays in *The Humanity of God* reveal Karl Barth's way of thought better than any other means short of reading his immense work, *Church Dogmatics*. In the first he explains why he reacted against nineteenth-century theology, in the second he looks back over forty years of his own work and calls for a new change of direction, and in the last he discusses the extent to which a Christian enjoys the freedom of action.

KARL BARTH

THE HUMANITY
OF GOD

COLLINS

THE FONTANA LIBRARY
THEOLOGY AND PHILOSOPHY

First published by Collins 1961
First issued in the Fontana Library 1967

These essays were originally published as three separate mono-graphs in the " Theologische Studien" series by Evangelischer Verlag A. G., Zollikon-Zurich

© *C. D. Deans 1960*
(*John Knox Press, Richmond 9, Virginia*)
First published in Great Britain 1961

Printed in Great Britain
Collins Clear-Type Press
London and Glasgow

CONTENTS

TRANSLATORS' PREFACE

The three essays by Karl Barth drawn together in this volume speak very well for themselves. It may be useful, however, to point out why they are being made available at this time in English.

First of all, the essays contain a concise and recent treatment of some of the central issues in Barth's theology, or for that matter in any Christian theology. This is especially true in the case of *The Humanity of God* and *The Gift of Freedom* which outline Barth's approach to Christology and to ethics respectively. Both of these areas are treated by him much more thoroughly in various parts of his *Church Dogmatics*, but the sheer length of that work may rather limit its reading audience even though it is now appearing in English. Hence it is hoped that the publication of these shorter writings will make more widely accessible some of the basic emphases in the recent and most mature form of Barth's theology.

In addition to the importance of their subject matter these essays are significant in that they reflect a certain development in Barth's thinking. The mere *fact* of this development needs to be underscored. In America and in Britain, Barth's theology is often understood and judged primarily on the basis of some of his earlier writings available in English. It is no longer possible, however, to think and speak responsibly about him if one's knowledge is limited to the earlier writings. The three essays published here illustrate in brief form both the fact and the direction of the development in Barth's thought.

The first of these essays, *Evangelical Theology in the 19th*

Century, reminds us that Barth has always had tremendous respect for the past, and that he has worked out his own theology in continuous dialogue with the Christian thinkers of preceding ages. In particular, it presents a recent and concise interpretation and appraisal by him of the theology against which he and his colleagues revolted in the second decade of our century. This retrospective view provides an excellent introduction to the next essay, *The Humanity of God*, in which Barth in 1956 looks back across some forty years of his own theological work and appraises the reaction against 19th-century liberal theology in which he himself was the most distinguished leader. In undiminished appreciation of both the need and the nature of this revolt, Barth sounds the call for a new change of direction in evangelical theology, hardly, if at all, less radical than that which took place just after the First World War. With honesty and forthrightness he asserts the need for correction of the extremes to which he and his colleagues went in their early development of the *Theology of the Word*. The key to this new change he finds in a deeper understanding of Christology and its implications. In the third essay, *The Gift of Freedom*, Barth proposes an approach to evangelical ethics which proceeds from the fact that God has made man free by choosing him to be his creature, partner, and child. He opposes ethics which merely sets up rules to be applied in a given situation. The purpose of evangelical ethics is to interpret not a set of rules but the gift of freedom, and in particular the call to human action which is implied in the gift.

John Newton Thomas
Thomas Wieser

EVANGELICAL THEOLOGY IN

THE NINETEENTH CENTURY[1]

"Theology," in the literal sense, means the science and doctrine of God. A very precise definition of the Christian endeavour in this respect would really require the more complex term "The-anthropology." For an abstract doctrine of God has no place in the Christian realm, only a "doctrine of God and of man," a doctrine of the commerce and communion between God and man.

"Evangelical" means informed by the gospel of Jesus Christ, as heard afresh in the 16th-century Reformation by direct return to Holy Scripture.

"Evangelical theology" must thus be understood as the science and doctrine of the commerce and communion between God and man, informed by the gospel of Jesus Christ as heard in Holy Scripture.

Evangelical theology according to this definition did exist in the 19th century. As part of the "panorama" of this era, along with much natural science and technology, history and politics, literature, art and philosophy, and along with Roman Catholic theology, this evangelical theology was present. My task here is to describe it briefly. I shall confine myself to the German-speaking world. This is justified in that 19th-century German theology was the signpost for theological endeavour elsewhere. This pre-eminence may not last indefinitely.

[1] This address, translated by Thomas Wieser, was given by Karl Barth at the meeting of the *Goethegesellschaft* in Hanover, 8th January, 1957, and entitled "Panorama of a Century."

9

The 19th century is behind us. So also is the evangelical theology of that century. The breach separating us from the 19th century is perhaps more pronounced in the field of theology than in any other academic discipline, although it is nowhere absent. This is not to say that 19th-century theology is to be dismissed. Such a procedure would be out of order in any academic discipline, but most certainly in theology. Theology belongs to the wider realm of the Christian Church, ecumenical and universal, in space as well as in time. In the Church there exists a community of concern that may be endangered, but never cancelled out, by even the most serious differences in approach. In the Church and hence in theology the commandment, " Honour thy father and thy mother," is valid, and this commandment remains binding on the children even when they have left their parents' house. To respect and sustain the ties that bind the present to the past, in spite of deep breaches, is therefore imperative. Evangelical theology of to-day has additional and for us more urgent tasks than those of the 19th century. But the 19th century's tasks remain for us, too. However different our approach, we cannot and must not abandon these tasks of a bygone day. To do so does not, I suppose, serve the purpose of any discipline; it certainly does not serve theology well.

Let us begin with some summary remarks about the history of evangelical theology in the 19th century.

There is hardly any doubt that the distinctive beginnings of 19th-century theology coincide with the publication of Schleiermacher's book *On Religion, Speeches to Its Cultured Despisers* in 1799. Whoever wishes to know and to understand this theology must read this little book with great care, though it is by no means easily digested. It clearly shows the breach separating the new theology at that time from both 17th-century Orthodoxy and 18th-century Enlightenment and Pietism.

The *course* of the history of 19th-century theology is fairly obvious from there on, at least in its main outline. In its understanding of Christian man, this theology was first animated and nourished by Herder and the Romantics, as well as by the religious and national awakening of the Napoleonic era. Subsequently, it found its splendid foundation and means of expression through speculative Idealism, through Hegel's version of it in particular, even though it came to be subjected to severe criticism from this very source. Under the increasing pressure of advancing positivism in the second half of the century—here the name of Albrecht Ritschl is to be remembered—theology retreated to the epistomology and ethics of Kant rediscovered, and to an interpretation of Luther rediscovered in the light of Kant. Finally, only a small realm remained for the genuine religious experience of the individual. Theology turned into philosophy of the history of religion in general, and of the Christian religion in particular.

The 19th century also had its outsiders. I mention Johann Christoph Blumhardt, Hermann Friedrich Kohlbrügge, Wilhelm Löhe and, for the final years, the quite different Franz Overbeck. Perhaps Johann Tobias Beck and Adolf Schlatter should be included here. These outsiders fitted only partially or not at all into the main development. Since they were either overlooked or viewed with condescension by their contemporaries, they in no way halted or even interrupted the main course. Kierkegaard in particular did not have the slightest influence on 19th-century theology, except, again, in the case of a few individuals. True, there was a more conservative element which was tied more strictly to the Bible and the traditional teachings of the Church; there was also a more progressive element, more liberal in its relationship to those authorities; furthermore, there were between them a number of theologies of mediation. But these elements were variations within the same general trend. None of them broke up the rather uniform picture even though there were occasional violent clashes. Incidentally, the theological leadership came undoubtedly from among the liberals. It was the liberals who raised the questions and answered them in a way which was characteristic for the century as a whole.

It may be much more difficult to come to an agreement as to the *eclipse* of this theology. The year 1900 brought the 19th century to its chronological end and marked at the same time a climax in the history of its theology : the publication of Harnack's *What is Christianity?* Due to this achievement, 19th-century theology continued to live for some time with force and dignity almost unbroken, in spite of signs of dissolution. This made possible a short-lived and partial renaissance of Schleiermacher around 1910. The actual end of the 19th century as the " good old days " came for theology as for everything else with the fateful year of 1914. Accidentally or not, a significant event took place during that very year. Ernst Troeltsch, the well-known professor of systematic theology and the leader of the then most modern school, gave up his chair in theology for one in philosophy. One day in early August 1914 stands out in my personal memory as a black day. Ninety-three German intellectuals impressed public opinion by their proclamation in support of the war policy of Wilhelm II and his counsellors. Among these intellectuals I discovered to my horror almost all of my theological teachers whom I had greatly venerated. In despair over what this indicated about the signs of the time I suddenly realised that I could not any longer follow either their ethics and dogmatics or their understanding of the Bible and of history. For me at least, 19th-century theology no longer held any future. For many, if not for most people, this theology did not become again what it had been, once the waters of the flood descending upon us at that time had somewhat receded. Everything has its time. Evangelical theology in the true spirit and style of the 19th century continued to exist and some vestiges still remain. But in its former wholeness it is a cause which to-day is significantly represented by only a few. This is not to say that we do not owe it our most serious attention for our own sake and for the sake of the future. But it remains true that the history of this theology had its beginnings, its various peaks, and then also its end.

One respectful statement must be added immediately at this point. Time made it unusually difficult for this theology to be developed and get a hearing, let alone to get accepted, beyond its own proper realm in the various Protestant churches. Nineteenth-century theology was burdened with the heritage of the 18th century. There was an all-pervasive rationalism and a retreat of vital or would-be vital Christianity into undergrounds of many kinds. These factors, coupled with the emergence of obscure forms of religious fanaticism, led to a kind of secularism probably more pointed than the much praised or deplored secularism of to-day. In addition, theology was measured against the impressive achievements and personalities of the so-called classical era of German culture, philosophic and poetic; against the breathtaking political movements of the war of liberation 1813-15, followed by the years of revolution and restoration, the foundation-laying of the empires, and the subsequent repercussions of all these events down to World War I. Above all, theology was measured against the all-embracing triumphs of the natural sciences, of philosophy, of history, of modern technology, as well as against Beethoven, Wagner, and Brahms, Gottfried Keller and Theodor Fontane, Ibsen and Sudermann. What did theology have to say to this century— not to speak of the shadow of Goethe and Bismarck and Friedrich Nietzsche—with its many-sided interests busily and progressively occupied elsewhere, to readers of the *Gartenlaube*, of the *Daheim*, and later of the *Kunstwart*[2] who numbered among them the more or less zealous Christians? What did this theology have to offer to a man who gave no thought to eternity, surrounded as he was by the riches of his time; who was firmly grounded in unshakable self-assurance, as was the case with the average man of the 19th century? Such a man would take notice of theology only if and when it suited his own radical or reactionary purposes, but he had so many objections to it that his indifference occasionally turned into open aversion and hostility. Whatever one may think of the presuppositions, methods, and results of these 19th-century evangelical theologians, it was an act of intellectual and, in the last analysis, of spiritual steadfastness that they were not afraid to face this modern man. They did so much more directly than their Roman Catholic counterparts because they dared to expose themselves to this climate as they carried through their work. This achievement must be seen and acknowl-

[2] *Kunstwart, Gartenlaube,* and *Daheim* were German weeklies or monthlies for art and literature.

edged before we disagree with these theologians and
depart from their positions.

One must speak with equal reverence of the human
and scientific attitude of many if not all of the repre-
sentatives of this theology. From Schleiermacher and his
melancholy friend De Wette in Basel down to Richard
Rothe, Isaak August Dorner, Ferdinand Christian Baur,
Hoffman and Frank of Erlangen, Alexander Schweizer
and Alois Emanuel Biedermann in Zurich, to Martin
Kaehler, Ludwig Ihmels, Adolf von Harnack, Wilhelm
Herrmann, and finally to the last great liberal, Hermann
Lüdemann, who was driven from Holstein and went to
Berne—what scholarly figures they were, each in his
own way, educated and cultivated, well grounded and
well rounded! Those of us who knew some of them
will know what I mean when I say that from many of
these persons emanated an unforgettable air of consci-
entiousness, of churchly and spontaneous piety, of a
peculiar combination of ethical earnestness and academic
dignity. All this exists to-day only in weak imitations
and as such might better not exist at all. I say this in
order to emphasise that in dealing with the theologians
of the 19th century, at least with the best among them,
we are faced with a type of person that merits our
highest respect. This in itself is reason enough for
our listening to them even to-day. Another question is
then certainly in order : whether these theologians may
not have been a little too serious at being professors,
taking themselves too seriously. Serenity is not the
strongest impression we gain from their writings, and
while several had a sense of humour it easily became a
trifle bilious when it was allowed to assert itself outside
their private life. In contrast to their strong scientific
self-assurance, a silent anxiety and oppression seems to

pervade the physical and mental picture of more than
one of them. This should not be a reproach. We have
lived through harder times, have endured worse things
than they did, and we are thereby, strangely enough,
made more free. We are removed from certain battles
and involvements in which they were caught in the
course of their opposition to and conversation with their
apparently sunny age. We can breathe more freely,
just because the air has become more raw. Modern
man can no longer impress us, as he impressed them,
in the light of his performances in this century. In the
midst of so much happily rambling and triumphant
idealism, materialism, naturalism, scepticism, and other
so-called realisms, one can easily become melancholy,
and the evangelical theologians probably did as well as
they could at that time, both as persons and as scholars.

I shall now turn to a necessarily sketchy survey of
the most important and significant problems 19th-
century theology had to face. What problems were
foremost in the minds of the theologians during all
phases of 19th-century development, and how did they
master them?

The key problem arose from the conviction that the
guiding principle of theology must be confrontation with
the contemporary age and its various conceptions, self-
understandings, and self-evidences, its genuine and less
genuine "movements," its supposed or real progress.
True, theology was also at work in and for the Church;
it was also concerned with its own proper centre, the
gospel of Jesus Christ and the faith responding to it;
it was concerned with searching and explaining the
Scriptures as the document of this gospel, with the history of the Church, founded and determined by this
gospel, with her doctrine and her life, with intellectual

and systematic formulation of Biblical truth, and with seeking and finding new ways of proclaiming it. However, the theologians had their eyes fixed on the world, and their thinking was necessarily conditioned by this outlook. They wrestled with the challenging issues of their times. Theology—and this was its strength—exposed itself to the world, as its most outstanding spokesmen and achievements demonstrate. Obviously theology has always been to some extent open towards and related to the world, consciously or unconsciously. It should be so. Retreats behind Chinese Walls never served theology well. It must be engaged in conversation with the contemporary world, whatever the means of the dialogue. Whoever denies this may read Schleiermacher, De Wette, Richard Rothe, and study the volumes of the *Christliche Welt*, edited by Martin Rade! The lazy man may learn thereby what openmindedness is! In this respect evangelical theology of the 19th century set an example never to be ignored in any vital theology.

Theology, however, went overboard—and this was its weakness—insofar as confrontation with the contemporary age was its *decisive* and *primary* concern. This was true not only, as happened so often, when it addressed the outside world *ex professo*, in the form of so-called apologetics, but also when it dealt with the questions most proper to itself. Theology never failed to react, whether approvingly or disapprovingly, critically or uncritically, to impulses from outside, at times even with extreme nervousness. This openness to the world meant (1) that through the open windows and doors came so much stimulation for thought and discussion that there was hardly time or love or zeal left for the task to be accomplished within the house itself. With all its ener-

gies captivated by the world, 19th-century theology
achieved surprisingly little in terms of a new and positive understanding of Christian truth and truths in
themselves, a primary necessity at all times. The winds
were enthusiastically welcomed and allowed to enter
freely through the outside doors. This meant (2) that
not a few doors inside were slammed which should have
been kept open as well. Nineteenth-century theology
ascribed normative character to the ideas of its environment. Consequently it was forced to make reductions
and oversimplifications, to indulge in forgetfulness and
carelessness, when it dealt with the exciting and all-
important matters of Christian understanding. These
developments were bound to threaten, indeed to under-
mine, both theology and the Church with impoverish-
ment and triviality. The outside winds brought not
merely fresh air, but also notoriously foul air. This
meant (3) that fatal errors blew in, were admitted, and
made themselves at home. These errors, far from being
simply tolerated, enjoyed birthright, even authority.
Countereffects to be sure were not lacking, but there
was no fundamental agreement about the absolute
primacy of the positive tasks of theology in and for
the Church, over against the secondary tasks of relating
to the various philosophies of the times. Finally, we
miss a certain carefree and joyful confidence in the
self-validation of the basic concerns of theology, a trust
that the most honest commerce with the world might
best be assured when the theologians, unheeding the
favours or disfavours of this world, confronted it with
the results of theological research carried out for its
own sake. It did not enter their minds that respectable
dogmatics could be good apologetics. Man in the 19th
century might have taken the theologians more seriously

if they themselves had not taken him so seriously. Even the best representatives of this theology have never overcome this limitation, in spite of their exemplary openness to the world. And this was the key problem of 19th-century theology.

This general assumption of openness to the world led necessarily to the specific assumption that theology could defend its own cause only within the framework of a total view of man, the universe, and God which could command universal recognition. How could the theologians establish and preserve the much-coveted contact with the contemporary world if they did not speak from within one of the current philosophies and world views, granted certain reservations and modifications? The validity of the Christian message was at stake, or more precisely the possibility of a voluntary but universal acceptance of its validity. Theoretically, Protestantism has always maintained that no outward or inward pressure can or should be brought upon anyone to accept the Christian message and with it the Christian faith. While this had often been overlooked in practice by Protestantism in earlier centuries, it had rightly become commonplace for the theologians of the 19th as well as the 18th century. Quite rightly these theologians stressed the possibility of free response offered to all men, including their contemporaries. We can only do justice to the fundamental significance of their efforts if we understand them against the background of the missionary and evangelistic concern which is characteristic of modern Christianity: the Christian obligation rediscovered in the 18th century to call and invite all men, near and far, to the free acceptance of the validity of the message of Jesus Christ and thus to faith in Him. So far, so good.

The theologians of the 19th century proceeded fundamentally along the lines of the 18th-century Christian Enlightenment. Their particular venture became questionable, however, as they set out to prove the possibility of faith in its relatedness to, and its conditioning by, the world views which were normative for their contemporaries and even for themselves. More precisely, they tried to find that point of reference in the world views where voluntary acceptance of the Christian message and the Christian faith suggested themselves more or less convincingly and were viewed at least as possibilities. It is evident that for this purpose the theologians had to make a particular world view their own and had to affirm its validity. This was all the easier for them as acceptance of a prevailing philosophy was precisely the presupposition for their work. The world views changed in the course of the century; but there were always theologians who went along, more or less convinced, if not enthusiastic, and who started the theological task afresh within the new framework.

In contrast to Enlightenment theology, the 19th-century theologians focused their attention on one particular point in relation to all the various world views of their time : man's supposedly innate and essential capacity to "sense and taste the infinite" as Schleiermacher said, or the "religious *a priori*" as later affirmed by Troeltsch. There was scarcely a theologian who did not also consider himself a professional philosopher. These philosophers of religion, more or less faithful or sophisticated advocates of one of the current world views, were busily working out a general epistomology, a system of metaphysics and ethics focusing on this very capacity. In these terms they sought to validate the potential for religion, including the Christian faith. The great efforts undertaken in the steps of Schleiermacher by men like De Wette, Biedermann, Lipsius, Kaftan, and Lüdemann were highly commendable.

And yet these efforts were surrounded by two questions which we may find difficult to answer in the affirmative.

First : Were men prepared to take such lessons from the theologians? Did they permit having their world views supplemented? Were they sensitive to man's openness towards religion and the Christian faith, and desirous to make any use of it? The revelation theology of Schelling during his later years should not be forgotten at this point. And we must not overlook that later philosophers like Lotze, Siebeck, Dilthey, and Eucken actively shared in their own way in the work of the theologians. But it was a bad omen that Goethe either ignored or viewed with displeasure what was happening. He disliked Schleiermacher's *Speeches*, quite apart from their romantic garb. The same can be said of Hegel, the other great master of the century. The efforts of Schleiermacher and of his successors did not acquire any significance for the broad mass of the " cultured " to whom Schleiermacher had addressed himself so impressively with his proof of the roots of religion in the structure of man's spiritual life. The thinking of the awakening labour class of the 19th century was even less influenced. The response to the efforts of the theologians was really not encouraging. If this does not necessarily speak against the excellence of what these philosopher-theologians did, it is yet a quite serious matter when compared with the explicit intention of their work.

The second question is more serious. Could the

Christian message and the Christian faith be a subject
for debate while the validity of a general world view
was presupposed? Is there any proof that acceptance
of a particular world view will make Christianity generally accessible or even possible? Even granted the
existence of man's religious disposition, can the Christian
faith be called one of its expressions, in other words a
"religion"? Nineteenth-century evangelical theology
assumed that it was so. But it could not do so without
subjugating the Christian message and the Christian
faith to that interpretation and form by which Christianity could achieve validity and general accessibility
for the proponents of the prevailing world view. The
Christian faith had to be understood as a "religion" if
it was to be generally accepted as valid. What if it
resisted this classification? What if acceptance was so
eagerly sought that Christian faith ceased to be Christian
faith as soon as it was interpreted as "religion"? What
if the attempt to give it the "firm" basis actually
removed the real ground from under it? Nineteenth-
century theology did not raise these questions. One
wonders, therefore, whether its most typical spokesmen
were not primarily philosophers and only secondarily
theologians. This might explain the failure of their
missionary task at a deeper level. Was it possible to
win the "Gentile" point of view, in order to commend
to them the Christian cause? Could this procedure
impress the "Gentiles"? Would it not have been
necessary first to be innocent as doves in order to be
wise as serpents?

Nineteenth-century theology worked on the general
assumption that relatedness to the world is its primary
task and on the specific assumption that there is a
possibility for general acceptance of the Christian faith.

The result was that the theologians, when they came to work on their proper task in and for the Church, were more interested in the Christian faith than in the Christian message. In terms of content they were more interested in man's relationship to God than in God's dealings with man, or, to quote the well-known term of Melanchthon, more in the *beneficia Christi* than in Christ Himself. This emphasis informed their interpretation of the Bible, their positive or critical attitude towards the early dogmas, and the confessions of the Reformation. It informed their research in, and their exposition of, church history and finally their own formulation of the Christian faith. The interest of these theologians focused on the believing man in his past and in his present, in his confrontation and association with Jesus Christ. Theological discussion with the contemporary world centred around the existence of the believing man, and in philosophy of religion particularly around the possibility of this existence. The prevailing interest in this direction would not necessarily have been erroneous had it been a matter of shift in tone and emphasis for serious and pertinent reasons. The Bible speaks emphatically of the commerce of the believing Israelite and the believing Christian with God and therefore of the believing man as such. How else could it testify on behalf of Him who was very God and very man? The theologians should not have hesitated so long to appeal to Luther, especially the early Luther, and to the early Melanchthon! And how much assistance and guidance could they have received had they paid any attention to Kierkegaard! There is no reason why the attempt of Christian anthropocentrism should not be made, indeed ought not to be made. There is certainly a place for legitimate Christian thinking starting from below and moving up, from man who is taken hold of by God to God who takes hold of man. Let us interpret this attempt by the 19th-century theologians in its best light! Provided that it in no way claims to be exclusive and absolute, one might well understand it as an attempt to formulate a theology of the third article of the Apostles' Creed, the Holy Spirit. If it had succeeded in this, 19th-century theology could have irrevocably stressed once again the fact that we cannot consider God's commerce with man without concurrently considering man's commerce with God. Theology is in reality not only the doctrine of God, but the doctrine of God and man. Interpreted in this light, 19th-century theology would not have forgotten or even suppressed, but rather stressed, the fact that man's relation to God is based on God's dealings with man, and not conversely. Starting from below, as it were, with Christian man, it could and should have struggled its way upward to an authentic explication of the Christian faith. It could and should have sought increasingly to validate the Christian message as God's act and word, the ground, object, and content of faith.

Hoffman of Erlangen, a Lutheran, must have had such an upswing in his mind when he made the daring attempt to portray the movement from man to God in the whole Bible and to get at the Scriptures as testimony of the divinely initiated and governed history leading to the ultimate salvation of man (*Heilsgeschichte*). He did this in terms of his selfconsciousness as a Christian. But insofar as Hoffman's theology was intended to be a theology of Christian self-understanding and not a theology of the Holy Spirit, it could not break through the general trend of the century. This is true in spite of the significance which this theology has for us even to-day. The basic concern of evangelical theology could not find a genuine expression in these terms. If only the need for an approach from below had been genuine and had grown out of a new examination of the authentic concerns of theology! However, it unabashedly originated from borrowed presuppositions. This movement of thought from man to God became exclusive and absolute. Nineteenth-century theologians spoke of "faith," and we do well to trust that they meant Christian faith. But their assumptions compelled them to understand faith as the realisation of one form of man's spiritual life and self-awareness. The more serious they were in this interpretation, the more the Christian faith appeared to be a windowless monad, dependent on human feelings, knowledge, and will. Like these, faith was supposed to be self-nurturing, self-governing, and self-sufficient. A capacity for the infinite within the finite, faith had no ground, object, or content other than itself. It had no *vis-à-vis*. Faith as the Christian's commerce with God could first and last be only the Christian's commerce with himself. It could express only itself, its own inner dialectics, in so many words and sentences. How could the truth of the Christian gospel be asserted except by understanding it and interpreting it as a statement, an expression, a predicate, or a symbol of the Christian's inner experience? Theology was still being penalised for accepting the Renaissance discovery that man was the measure of all things, including Christian things. On this ground the testimony of Christian faith, however honest, and however richly endowed with Biblical and Reformation recollections, could only exist like a fish out of water. On this ground there was no effective answer to be given to Feuerbach who eagerly invoked Luther's sanction in support of his theory that statements of the Christian faith, like those of all other religions, are in reality statements of more or less profound human needs and desires projected into the infinite. Christian dogmatics was especially hard put during this period to raise any interesting and provocative questions, and to provide vital answers. By the time it had dealt with the philosophical presuppositions and the historical-critical problems, its voice was subdued and bare of enthusiasm. Was it at all worth the trouble publicly to discuss a man's inner experiences even, if he was a Christian? Was such a self-revelation on the basis of self-knowledge at all possible? May not man be more hidden from man, the Christian from other Christians, than God is hidden from man? These questions, too, were among those which 19th-century theology never raised because it saw no problem in this direction.

However, theology could hardly improve its position among the other academic disciplines, much as it so desired, as long as it could give as the reason for its particular existence merely a specific human self-understanding and expression. Another consequence of this religious anthropocentrism was even worse. It has already been said that when the Christian gospel was changed into a statement, a religion, about Christian self-awareness, the God was lost sight of who in His sovereignty confronts man, calling him to account, and dealing with him as Lord. This loss also blurred the sight horizontally. The Christian was condemned to uncritical and irresponsible subservience to the patterns, forces, and movements of human history and civilisation. Man's inner experience did not provide a firm enough ground for resistance to these phenomena. Deprived of a guiding principle man could turn anywhere. It was fatal for the evangelical Church and for Christianity in the 19th century that theology in the last analysis had nothing more to offer than the "human," the "religious," mystery and its noncommittal "statements," leaving the faithful to whatever impressions and influences from outside proved strongest.

How confused was the position of the evangelical Church in regard to changing world views! How long did it take the Church to become concerned about social questions, to take socialism seriously, and with how much spiritual dilettantism was this finally done! How naïvely did the Church subscribe to political conservatism in the first half of the century and in the second half to the preservation of the liberal bourgeoisie, the growing nationalism and militarism! All this certainly not with ill will; but theologically the ship was without a rudder. And he who in 1933 may still have been spellbound by the theology of the 19th century was hopelessly condemned, save for a special intervention of grace, to bet on the wrong horse in regard to national socialism and during the clash between the Confessing Church and the German Christians who supported the new régime (*Kirchenkampf*). I mention these developments only as symptoms. As indications of the situation brought about by the religious anthropocentrism of 19th-century theology they needed mentioning.

I would like to make some final remarks. Mindful of its origins in Herder and the Romanticists, 19th-century theology has given new emphasis and recognition to the essentially historical nature of the Christian faith which sets Christianity apart from other religions. This is the merit and achievement of this theology. Christian faith is shaped by its relationship to the history which finds its central meaning in the name of Jesus Christ. For this very reason Biblical exegesis and the study of

the history of the Church and its dogmas were bound
to become again urgent and distinctive tasks. The path
to be followed in this attempt to do justice to the
historicity of Christianity was irrevocably given by the
presuppositions upon which 19th-century theology oper-
ated. Its spokesmen had no choice but to understand
the Christian faith, in its essence, as a series of historical
phenomena : Christianity a particular religion alongside
other religions and in the context of the general history
of religions; past patterns and expressions of Christianity;
and finally the history which finds its central meaning in
the name of Jesus Christ, His person and His life, the
original phenomenon of faith so to speak, but never more
than a *historical* phenomenon. The theologians had to
apprehend Him—or should we say, to lay hold of Him?
—historically, that is in terms of the history of religions
and according to the historical-critical method prevailing
at that time. They had to approach the person and
the life of Jesus on the basis of the New Testament
record, but they also had to distinguish His own religion
from that of His witnesses and their environment.
Furthermore, they had to establish and to evaluate
these corollary religious events, both in their particular
characteristics and in their relationship to the original
event of Jesus Christ. They had to trace the forms of
faith in the Church down through the centuries in their
variety and in their continuing development. Informed
by the results of this research, they had to ascertain
the contemporary form of Christian faith. In this
historical-critical undertaking, 19th-century theology
enjoyed without reservation the confrontation and the
formal agreement with the conceptions and ways of
thought of the environment. Theology met the test as a
science, and brilliantly so in the life work of men—to

again mention only a few—like Ferdinand Christian
Baur, Karl August von Hase, Heinrich Julius Holtzmann,
Adolf Jülicher, Adolf von Harnack, Karl Holl, Ernst
Troeltsch; one should also remember to give honour to
Theodor Zahn, on the conservative side. In the light
of the general and of the specific assumptions of 19th-
century theology, the historical determination of the
Christian faith became visible in the results of the
research of these men. These results were constantly
vacillating, contested, and subject to discussion, and
some were truly amazing and caused vexation or rejoic-
ing, depending on one's outlook. I remember for instance
when I was a student at Berne, Rudolf Steck, one of the
very dignified last disciples of the so-called Tübingen
School, suggesting, if not teaching, that not only several
of the Pauline letters, but every one of them, might be
"false," might be products of the second century. And
we all know of the famous *Life of Jesus* by David
Friedrich Strauss who gave one of the strongest impulses
to the theological enterprise by his attempt to prove the
mythical character of even the Christ phenomenon!
Even in the cautious and moderate research of the
majority of the scholars along the main roads there was
curtailing, rationalising, psychologising, and demytholo-
gising going on!

Important for the total picture, however, were not the
sometimes more radical, sometimes more conservative,
results of this research, but rather the fundamental
questions which were triumphantly bypassed. Was Jesus
Christ really nothing more than the original phenomenon
of Christian faith? Was He not to be comprehended
as its ground, content, and object on the basis of the
first records—the New Testament—as well as of the
later accounts—those of the Church—varied and condi-

tioned by their time as they were? Was, therefore, Christ's historical existence at all accessible to a research which reached beyond the texts of the New Testament? What if the structure of these texts disqualified them as a proper " source " for use by neutral historical science? This question was persistently raised by Martin Kaehler in the 19th century, but it received no attention. Furthermore, were the theologians not doomed to misread the New Testament texts in their attempt at understanding them as documents of certain religious phenomena? Finally, with this purpose in mind could they possibly expect to understand the documents of Church history and of the history of doctrine? Was this endeavour truly what it claimed to be, a genuinely historical one? Did not the whole enterprise, from beginning to end, painfully suffer from the fundamental mistake that, in the words of Schleiermacher, productive theologising was possible only from a lofty place " above " Christianity? What if by talking about Christianity as a religion these theologians had already ceased to speak of Christianity and hence were unable to communicate the faith with authority to those on the outside? What if the only relevant way of speaking of Christianity was from within? We do not fail to pay due tribute to the "historical-critical " theology for the valuable stimulation, illumination, and guidance it offered with regard to the Bible and Church history. But it did so only insofar as it was not merely a "historical-critical " method but was *nolens volens* theology, above all insofar as its *subject matter* was powerful enough to break through the questionable vehicles of 19th-century research and speak for itself. Except for this fact, since otherwise it was nothing more than "historical-critical " research and doctrine, forsaken

by God and the Spirit, 19th-century theology would not
have been able to offer any Christian truth of importance and of historical relevancy. If it had been allowed
to run its full course, the Christian faith would no
longer have been subjected to the history which finds its
central meaning in the name of Jesus Christ. On the
contrary, this history would have become subjected to
the interpretation by the particular mode of Christian
religion which the theologians equated with the Christian
faith.

A deplorable consequence must be mentioned with
reference to this last point. Nineteenth-century theology
appeared to the outside world mainly as history of
religion. This may have been the reason for the mutual
indifference which existed, at least during the second
half of the century, between evangelical theology and
Roman Catholic theology. It is debatable whether this
indifference was an improvement over the vivid and so
much complained-about hostilities of earlier times which
at least indicated mutual interest. Roman Catholic
theology, too, underwent strange developments in the
beginning of the century, and these were in part strikingly
similar to those of Protestantism. However, in the era
of Pius IX it regained its peculiar balance through a far
from exemplary return to Thomism. Obviously evangelical theology, considered as a discipline of the history
of religion, had no choice but to interpret the conduct of
its opponent as an uncritical and unhistorical dealing
with authority and hence reminiscent of the Dark Ages.
Conversely, Roman Catholic theology had to condemn
the endeavour of evangelical theology as irresponsible
surrender and secularisation of the historical character
of the Christian faith. A dialogue between these two
partners which would have gone beyond the shouting

back and forth of slogans was as impossible as a conversation between an elephant and a whale. The relationship did not even take the form of meaningful polemics, let alone the willingness to listen to one another, to learn from one another, to seek and to maintain the ecumenical contacts within the limits of the possible. Who among the evangelicals ever read Catholic dogmatics—and which Roman Catholic ever looked into our expositions of the faith, our *"Glaubenslehren"*? No wonder that both partners turned their backs on each other with the gesture and the prayer of thanksgiving of the Pharisee in the Temple. Could and should this go on? If history of religion on our side (and Neo-Thomism on the other) was the last word of wisdom, the indifference was bound to continue.

I am at the end. It has been my task to give a report on the evangelical theology in the 19th century. Therefore, I was not and I am not now under any obligation to tell you, or even to indicate, how this history continued. It would be interesting to hear what a wiser man than myself will have to say about its development a hundred years from now. The history did go on. There is even a certain continuity in spite of inevitable discontinuity. I repeat : the 19th century is *not* to be dismissed, nor is its theology. I could not follow the rule *De mortuis nihil nisi bonum* (speak nothing but good of the dead) simply because the theologians of that time are not dead. "In Him they all have life," in the greatness and within the limitations in which they once lived. *Et lux perpetua luceat eis* (and the eternal light shines upon them.) And thus they live, excitingly enough, also for us. They will not cease to speak to us. And we cannot cease to listen to them.

THE HUMANITY OF GOD[1]

The humanity of God! Rightly understood that is
bound to mean God's relation to and turning towards
man. It signifies the God who speaks with man in
promise and command. It represents God's existence,
intercession, and activity for man, the intercourse God
holds with him, and the free grace in which He wills to
be and is nothing other than the God of man.

Surely I do not deceive myself when I assume that
our theme to-day should suggest a *change of direction*[2]
in the thinking of evangelical theology. We are or
ought now to be engaged in this change, not in opposition to but none the less in *distinction* from an earlier
change. What began forcibly to press itself upon us
about forty years ago was not so much the humanity of
God as His *deity*—a God absolutely unique in His
relation to man and the world, overpoweringly lofty
and distant, strange, yes even wholly other. Such was the
God with whom man has to do when he takes the name
of God upon his lips, when God encounters him, when
he enters into relation with God. We were confronted
by the mystery comparable only to the impenetrable
darkness of death, in which God veils Himself precisely
when He unveils, announces, and reveals Himself to
man, and by the judgment man must experience because
God is gracious to him, because He wills to be and is
his God. What we discovered in the change which
occurred at that time was the majesty of the crucified,

[1] This lecture, translated by John Newton Thomas, was
delivered at the meeting of the Swiss Reformed Ministers'
Association in Arau, 25th September, 1956.
[2] German: *Wendung*.

so evident in its full horror, just as Grünewald saw and
depicted Him. We saw the finger of John the Baptist,
by the same artist, pointing with authority to this holy
One: "He must increase but I must decrease."

Unmistakably for us the *humanity* of God at that time
moved from the centre to the periphery, from the
emphasised subordinate clause to the less emphasised
subordinate clause. I should indeed have been somewhat
embarrassed if one had invited me to speak on the
humanity of God—say in the year 1920, the year in
which I stood up in this hall against my great teacher,
Adolf von Harnack. We should have suspected evil
implications in this topic. In any case we were not
occupied with it. That it is our subject for to-day
and that I could not refuse to say something on it
is a symptom of the fact that the earlier change of
direction was not the last word. It could not be. Simi-
larly, the change in which we are now engaged cannot
be the last word. That, however, may become the concern of another generation. Our problem is this: to
derive the knowledge of the humanity of God from
the knowledge of His deity.

I

Permit me to give my exposition of this theme first in
the form of a report. In a consideration of the earlier
change referred to above, a viewpoint regarding the
urgent task of the succeeding period and of to-day will
emerge.

The change of direction then made had a pronounced
critical and *polemic* character. It came to completion
gradually when viewed in terms of time, but as a sudden

conversion when viewed in terms of content. It was a precipitous break with the ruling theology of the time, a theology more or less liberal—or even orthodox—representing the climax of a development which had successfully asserted itself for two or three centuries, apparently incapable of being arrested.

We are called upon to-day to accord to that earlier theology, and the entire development culminating in it, greater historical justice than appeared to us possible and feasible in the violence of the first break-off and clash. This is an easier task to-day than it would have been earlier. However, even in the most unbiased evaluation of its legitimate purpose and its unmistakable service, even in the most peaceful review of it, one cannot hide the fact that it could no longer continue as it was. Modification of the theological conception then normative through new and at the same time older and original Christian knowledge and ways of speaking proved unavoidable. Evangelical theology almost all along the line, certainly in all its representative forms and tendencies, had become *religionistic, anthropocentric,* and in this sense *humanistic.* What I mean to say is that an external and internal disposition and emotion of man, namely his piety—which might well be Christian piety—had become its object of study and its theme. Around this it revolved and seemed compelled to revolve without release. This was true of evangelical theology in its doctrine of principles, in its presentation of the Christian past and its practical understanding of the Christian present, in its ethics and in that which perhaps was to be regarded as its dogmatics, in the proclamation and instruction of the Church determined by it—above all, however, in its interpretation of the Bible. What did it know and say of the *deity* of God? For this theology, to think about God meant to think in a scarcely veiled fashion about man, more exactly about the religious, the Christian religious man. To speak about God meant to speak in an exalted tone but once again and more than ever about this man—his revelations and wonders, his faith and his works. There is no question about it : here man was made great at the cost of God—the divine God who is someone other than man, who sovereignly confronts him, who immovably and unchangeably stands over against him as the Lord, Creator, and Redeemer. This God who is also man's free partner in a history inaugurated by Him and in a dialogue ruled by Him was in danger of being reduced, along with this history and this dialogue, to a pious notion—to a mystical expression and symbol of a current alternating between a man and his own heights or depths. But whatever truth was gained in this way could be only that of a monologue.

At this point some of us were appalled after we, along with everyone else, had drained the different chalices of this theology to the last drop. We then concluded (from approximately the middle of the second decade of our century on) that we could not side with it any longer. Why? Had the pious man and the religion of whose history and presence we had heard so many glorious things at the university and of which we ourselves thereafter had tried to speak, become a matter of question in our own person? Was it the encounter with socialism as interpreted by Kutter and Ragaz which opened our eyes to the fact that God might actually be wholly other than the God confined to the musty shell of the Christian-religious self-consciousness, and that as such He might act and speak? Was it the suddenly darkened outlook for the world, in contrast to the long period of peace in our youth, which awakened to us the fact that man's distress might be too great for a reference to his religious potentiality to prove a comforting and prophetic word? Was it—this has played a decisive role for me personally—precisely the failure of the ethics of the modern theology of the time, with the outbreak of the First World War, which caused us to grow puzzled also about its exegesis, its treatment of history, and its dogmatics? Or was it, in a positive sense, the message of Blumhardt concerning the Kingdom of God which, remarkably enough, was only then becoming timely? Was it Kierkegaard, Dostoevski, Overbeck, read as a commentary on that message, through which we found ourselves compelled to look for and set sail to new shores? Or was it something more fundamental than all that, namely, the discovery that the theme of the Bible, contrary to the critical and to the orthodox exegesis which we inherited, certainly could not be man's religion and religious morality and certainly not his own secret divinity? The stone wall we first ran up against was that the theme of the Bible is the deity of *God*, more exactly God's *deity*—God's independence and particular character, not only in relation to the natural but also to the spiritual cosmos; God's absolutely unique existence, might, and initiative, above all, in His relation to man. Only in this manner were we able to understand the voice of the Old and New Testaments. Only with this perspective did we feel we could henceforth be theologians, and in particular, preachers—ministers of the divine Word.

Were we right or wrong? We were certainly right! Let one read the doctrine of Troeltsch and Stephan. Let one read also the dogmatics of Lüdemann, in its way so solid, or even that of Seeberg. If all that wasn't

a blind alley! Beyond doubt what was then in order
was not some kind of further shifting around within
the complex of inherited questions, as this was finally
attempted by Wobbermin, Schaeder, and Otto, but
rather a change of direction. The ship was threatening
to run aground; the moment was at hand to turn the
rudder an angle of exactly 180 degrees. And in view
of what is to be said later, let it immediately be stated:
" That which is gone does not return." Therefore there
never could be a question of denying or reversing that
change. It was, however, later on and it is to-day a
question of "revision."[3] A *genuine* revision in no way
involves a subsequent retreat, but rather a new beginning and attack in which what previously has been said
is to be said more than ever, but now even better. If
that which we then thought we had discovered and
brought forth was no last word but one requiring a
revision, it was none the less a true word. As such it
must remain, and still cannot be bypassed; rather it
constitutes the presupposition of that which must be
further considered to-day. He who may not have joined
in that earlier change of direction, who still may not
be impressed with the fact that God is God, would
certainly not see what is now to be said in addition as
the true word concerning His humanity.

In regard to the change which then took place one
might well have sung:

> See the moon in yonder sky?
> 'Tis only half that meets the eye.[4]

---

[3] German: *Retraktation*, from the Latin, *retractatio*. Barth
is thinking of Augustine's *Retractationes*.

[4] From the hymn, *The Moon Has Risen*, by Matthius
Claudius.

It must now quite frankly be granted that we were at that time only partially in the right, even in reference to the theology which we inherited and from which we had to disengage ourselves—partially right in the same sense in which all preponderantly critical-polemic movements, attitudes, and positions, however meaningful they may be, are usually only partially in the right. What expressions we used—in part taken over and in part newly invented!—above all, the famous "wholly other" breaking in upon us "perpendicularly from above," the not less famous "infinite qualitative distinction" between God and man, the vacuum, the mathematical point, and the tangent in which alone they must meet. "And as she warbled, a thousand voices in the field sang it back."[5] There was also the bold assurance that there is in the Bible only *one* theological interest, namely, that in God; that only *one* way appears, namely, that from above downwards; that only *one* message can be heard, namely, that of an immediate forgiveness of sins both in prospect and in retrospect. The problem of ethics was identified with man's sickness unto death; redemption was viewed as consisting in the abolition of the creatureliness of the creature, the swallowing of immanence by transcendence, and in conformity with these the demand for a faith like a spring into the abyss, and more of the like. All this, however well it may have been meant and however much it may have mattered, was nevertheless said somewhat severely and brutally, and moreover—at least according to the other side—in part heretically. How we cleared things away! And we did almost nothing but clear away. Everything which even remotely smacked of mysticism and morality, of pietism and romanticism, or even of

[5] Emmanuel Geibel.

idealism, was suspected and sharply interdicted or bracketed with reservations which sounded actually prohibitive! What should really have been only a sad and friendly smile was a derisive laugh.

Did not the whole thing frequently seem more like the report of an enormous execution than the message of the Resurrection, which was its real aim? Was the impression of many contemporaries wholly unfounded, who felt that the final result might be to stand Schleiermacher on his head, that is, to make *God* great for a change at the cost of *man*? Were they wrong in thinking that actually not too much had been won and that perhaps in the final analysis it was only a new Titanism at work? Was it only obduracy when, beside the many who to some extent listened with relief and accompanied us, so many others preferred to shake their heads, nonplussed or—like Harnack at that time—even angry over such an innovation? Was there not perhaps in their obduracy the dark presentiment that, in the religionism, the anthropocentrism, the ill-fated humanism of the earlier theology, there might have been something at work that could not be given up? Is it possible that, granted the unmistakable contestability, even perversity of their position, the *humanity* of God did not quite come into its rights in the manner in which we, absorbed as we were in contemplation of the mighty deployment of Leviathan and Behemoth in the book of Job, lifted up His deity on the candlestick?

Where did we really go astray? Where was and is the starting point for the new change of direction? The shrewd friend from another shore[6] has, as is well known,

[6] Hans Urs von Balthasar, a Swiss Roman Catholic priest and author of *Karl Barth: A Presentation and Interpretation of His Theology.*

laid his finger on the fact that at that time we worked
almost exclusively with the concept of diastasis, only
seldom and incidentally with the complementary concept
of analogy. That may be the case. But was not this
formal principle merely a symptom of a more deep-
seated, essential infirmity in our thinking and speaking
at that time? I believe it consisted in the fact that we
were wrong exactly where we were right, that at first
we did not know how to carry through with sufficient
care and thoroughness the new knowledge of the *deity*
of God which was so exciting both to us and to others.
It was certainly good and proper to return to it and to
make it known with greater power. Moreover, Master
Calvin in particular has given us more than wise guidance
in this matter. The allegation that we were teaching
that God is everything and man nothing, was bad. As
a matter of fact, certain hymns of praise to humanism
were at that time occasionally raised—the Platonic in
particular, in which Calvin was nurtured.

It is nevertheless true that it was pre-eminently the
image and concept of a " wholly other " that fascinated
us and which we, though not without examination, had
dared to identify with the deity of Him who in the
Bible is called Yahweh-Kyrios. We viewed this " wholly
other " in isolation, abstracted and absolutised, and set
it over against man, this miserable wretch—not to say
boxed his ears with it—in such fashion that it con-
tinually showed greater similarity to the deity of the
God of the philosophers than to the deity of the God
of Abraham, Isaac, and Jacob. Was there not a threat
that a stereotyped image would arise again? What if
the result of the new hymn to the majesty of God should
be a new confirmation of the hopelessness of all human
activity? What if it should issue in a new justification of

the autonomy of man and thus of secularism in the
sense of the Lutheran doctrine of the two kingdoms?
That was the concern and the objection of Leonhard
Ragaz. God forbid! We did not believe nor intend
any such thing.

But did it not appear to escape us by quite a distance
that the *deity* of the *living* God—and we certainly
wanted to deal with Him—found its meaning and its
power only in the context of His history and of His
dialogue with *man*, and thus in His *togetherness* with
man? Indeed—and this is the point back of which we
cannot go—it is a matter of *God's* sovereign togetherness with man, a togetherness grounded in Him and
determined, delimited, and ordered through Him alone.
Only in this way and in this context can it take place
and be recognised. It is a matter, however, of God's
togetherness with man. Who God is and what He is
in His deity He proves and reveals not in a vacuum
as a divine being-for-Himself, but precisely and authen-
tically in the fact that He exists, speaks, and acts as
the *partner* of man, though of course as the absolutely
superior partner. He who does *that* is the living God.
And the freedom in which He does *that* is His deity.
It is the deity which as such also has the character of
humanity. In this and only in this form was—and
still is—our view of the deity of God to be set in
opposition to that earlier theology. There must be positive acceptance and not unconsidered rejection of the
elements of truth, which one cannot possibly deny to it
even if one sees all its weaknesses. It is precisely God's
deity which, rightly understood, includes his *humanity*.

II

How do we come to know that? What permits and
requires this statement? It is a *Christological* statement,
or rather one grounded in and to be unfolded from
Christology. A second change of direction after that
first one would have been superfluous had we from the
beginning possessed the presence of mind to venture the
whole inevitable counterthrow from the Christological
perspective and thus from the superior and more exact
standpoint of the central and entire witness of Holy
Scripture. Certainly in *Jesus Christ*, as He is attested
in Holy Scripture, we are not dealing with man in
the abstract : not with the man who is able with his
modicum of religion and religious morality to be sufficient
unto himself without God and thus himself to be God.
But neither are we dealing with *God* in the abstract :
not with one who in His deity exists only separated
from man, distant and strange and thus a non-human if
not indeed an inhuman God. In Jesus Christ there is
no isolation of man from God or of God from man.
Rather, in Him we encounter the history, the dialogue,
in which God and man meet together and are together,
the reality of the covenant *mutually* contracted, preserved, and fulfilled by them. Jesus Christ is in His
one Person, as true *God, man's* loyal partner, and as true
man, God's. He is the Lord humbled for communion
with man and likewise the Servant exalted to communion
with God. He is the Word spoken from the loftiest, most
luminous transcendence and likewise the Word heard
in the deepest, darkest immanence. He is both, without
their being confused but also without their being divided;

He is wholly the one and wholly the other. Thus in this oneness Jesus Christ is the Mediator, the Reconciler, between God and man. Thus He comes forward to *man* on behalf of *God* calling for and awakening faith, love, and hope, and to *God* on behalf of *man*, representing man, making satisfaction and interceding. Thus He attests and guarantees to man God's free *grace* and at the same time attests and guarantees to God man's free *gratitude*. Thus He establishes in His Person the justice of God *vis-à-vis* man and also the justice of man before God. Thus He is in His Person the covenant in its fullness, the Kingdom of heaven which is at hand, in which God speaks and man hears, God gives and man receives, God commands and man obeys, God's glory shines in the heights and thence into the depths, and peace on earth comes to pass among men in whom He is well pleased. Moreover, exactly in this way Jesus Christ, as this Mediator and Reconciler between God and man, is also the *Revealer* of them both. We do not need to engage in a free-ranging investigation to seek out and construct who and what God truly is, and who and what man truly is, but only to read the truth about both where it resides, namely, in the fullness of their togetherness, their covenant which proclaims itself in Jesus Christ.

Who and what *God* is—this is what in particular we have to learn better and with more precision in the new change of direction in the thinking and speaking of evangelical theology, which has become necessary in the light of the earlier change. But the question must be, who and what is God *in Jesus Christ*, if we here to-day would push forward to a better answer.

Beyond doubt God's *deity* is the first and fundamental fact that strikes us when we look at the existence of

Jesus Christ as attested in the Holy Scripture. And God's deity in Jesus Christ consists in the fact that God Himself in Him is the *subject* who speaks and acts with sovereignty. *He* is the free One in whom all freedom has its ground, its meaning, its prototype. *He* is the initiator, founder, preserver, and fulfiller of the covenant. *He* is the sovereign Lord of the amazing relationship in which He becomes and is not only different from man but also one with him. *He* is also the creator of him who is His partner. *He* it is through whose faithfulness the corresponding faithfulness of His partner is awakened and takes place. The old Reformed Christology worked that out especially clearly in its doctrine of the " hypostatic union " : God is on the throne. In the existence of Jesus Christ, the fact that God speaks, gives, orders, comes absolutely first—that man hears, receives, obeys, can and must only follow this first act. In Jesus Christ man's freedom is wholly enclosed in the freedom of God. Without the condescension of God there would be no exaltation of man. As the Son of God and not otherwise, Jesus Christ is the Son of Man. This sequence is irreversible. God's independence, omnipotence, and eternity, God's holiness and justice and thus God's deity, in its original and proper form, is the power leading to this effective and visible sequence in the existence of Jesus Christ : superiority preceding subordination. Thus we have here no universal deity capable of being reached conceptually, but this concrete deity—real and recognisable in the *descent* grounded in that sequence and peculiar to the existence of Jesus Christ.

But here there is something even more concrete to be seen. God's high freedom in Jesus Christ is His freedom for *love*. The divine capacity which operates and exhibits itself in that superiority and subordination is

manifestly also God's capacity to bend downwards, to
attach Himself to another and this other to Himself,
to be together with him. This takes place in that
irreversible sequence, but in it is completely real. In
that sequence there arises and continues in Jesus Christ
the highest communion of God with man. God's deity
is thus no prison in which He can exist only in and for
Himself. It is rather His freedom to be in and for
Himself but also with and for us, to assert but also to
sacrifice Himself, to be wholly exalted but also completely humble, not only almighty but also almighty
mercy, not only Lord but also servant, not only judge
but also Himself the judged, not only man's eternal
king but also his brother in time. And all that without
in the slightest forfeiting His deity! All that, rather,
in the highest proof and proclamation of His deity!
He who *does* and manifestly *can* do all that, He and no
other is the living God. So constituted is His deity, the
deity of the God of Abraham, Isaac, and Jacob. In
Jesus Christ it is in this way operative and recognisable.
If He is the Word of Truth, then the truth of *God* is
exactly this and nothing else.

It is when we look at Jesus Christ that we know
decisively that God's deity does not exclude, but includes
His *humanity*. Would that Calvin had energetically
pushed ahead on this point in his Christology, his
doctrine of God, his teaching about predestination, and
then logically also in his ethics! His Geneva would
then not have become such a gloomy affair. His letters
could then not have contained so much bitterness. It
would then not be so easy to play a Heinrich Pestalozzi
and, among his contemporaries, a Sebastian Castellio
off against him. How could God's deity exclude His

humanity, since it is God's freedom for love and thus
His capacity to be not only in the heights but also in
the depths, not only great but also small, not only in and
for Himself but also with another distinct from Him,
and to offer Himself to him? In His deity there is
enough room for communion with man. Moreover God
has and retains in His relation to this other one the
unconditioned priority. It is His act. *His* is and remains
the first and decisive Word, *His* the initiative, *His* the
leadership. How could we see and say it otherwise when
we look at Jesus Christ in whom we find man taken
up into communion with God? No, God requires no
exclusion of humanity, no non-humanity, not to speak
of inhumanity, in order to be truly God. But we may
and must, however, look further and recognise the fact
that actually His deity *encloses humanity in itself*. This
is not the fatal Lutheran doctrine of the two natures
and their properties. On the contrary, the essential aim
of this doctrine is not to be denied at this point but to
be adopted. It would be the false deity of a false God
if in His deity His humanity did not also immediately
encounter us. Such false deities are by Jesus Christ
once for all made a laughing stock. In Him the fact is
once for all established that God does not exist without
man.

It is not as though God stands in need of another as
His partner, and in particular of man, in order to be
truly God. "What is man, that thou art mindful of him,
and the son of man that thou dost care for him?" Why
should God not also be able, as eternal Love, to be
sufficient unto Himself? In His life as Father, Son, and
Holy Spirit He would in truth be no lonesome, no
egotistical God even without man, yes, even without the

whole created universe. And He must more than ever
be not *for* man; He *could*—one even thinks He *must*—
rather be against him. But that is the mystery in which
He meets us in the existence of Jesus Christ. He wants
in His freedom actually not to be without man but *with*
him and in the same freedom not against him but *for*
him, and that apart from or even counter to what man
deserves. He wants in fact to be man's partner, his
almighty and compassionate Saviour. He chooses to
give man the benefit of His power, which encompasses
not only the high and the distant but also the deep and
the near, in order to maintain communion with him
in the realm guaranteed by His deity. He determines to
love him, to be his God, his Lord, his compassionate
Preserver and Saviour to eternal life, and to desire his
praise and service.

In this divinely free volition and election, in this
sovereign decision (the ancients said, in His decree), God
is *human*. His free affirmation of man, His free concern
for him, His free substitution for him—this is God's
humanity. We recognise it exactly at the point where
we also first recognise His deity. Is it not true that in
Jesus Christ, as He is attested in the Holy Scripture,
genuine deity includes in itself genuine humanity?
There is the father who cares for his lost son, the king
who does the same for his insolvent debtor, the Samaritan
who takes pity on the one who fell among robbers and
in his thorough-going act of compassion cares for him
in a fashion as unexpected as it is liberal. And this is
the act of compassion to which all these parables as
parables of the Kingdom of heaven refer. The very
One who speaks in these parables takes to His heart
the weakness and the perversity, the helplessness and the

misery, of the human race surrounding Him. He does not despise men, but in an inconceivable manner esteems them highly just as they are, takes them in to His heart and sets Himself in their place. He perceives that the superior will of God, to which He wholly subordinates Himself, requires that He sacrifice Himself for the human race, and seeks His honour in doing this. In the mirror of this humanity of Jesus Christ the humanity of God enclosed in His deity reveals itself. Thus God is as He is. Thus He affirms man. Thus He is concerned about him. Thus He stands up for him. The God of Schleiermacher cannot show mercy. The God of Abraham, Isaac, and Jacob can and does. If Jesus Christ is the Word of Truth, the " mirror of the fatherly heart of God,"[7] then Nietzsche's statement that man is something that must be overcome is an impudent lie. Then the truth of God is, as Titus 3 :4 says, His loving-kindness and nothing else.

III

We should not yet, however, have arrived at this insight in the right way—in any case we should not yet have been certain of it—if its content had not been evident along the lines which all Christian thinking and speaking must follow. The statement regarding God's humanity, the Immanuel, to which we have advanced as a first step up from the Christological centre, cannot but have the most far-reaching consequences. These result from the fact that we are asked about the *correspondence*— here the concept of analogy may come into its right—

[7] Martin Luther.

of our thinking and speaking with the humanity of God.
The most fundamental and important of these consequences, though not all of them, must now be brought
more significantly to light.

From the fact that God is human in the sense described, there follows first of all a quite definite *distinction*
of *man* as such. It is a distinction of every being which
bears the human countenance. This includes the whole
stock of those capacities and possibilities which are in
part common to man and to other creatures, and in
part peculiar to him, and likewise man's work and his
productions. The acknowledgement of this distinction
has nothing to do with an optimistic judgment of man.
It is due him because he is the being whom God willed
to exalt as His covenant-partner, not otherwise. But
just because God is human in this sense, it is actually
due to man and may not be denied him through any
pessimistic judgment, whatever its basis. On the basis
of the eternal will of God we have to think of *every
human being*, even the oddest, most villainous or miserable, as one to whom Jesus Christ is Brother and God
is Father; and we have to deal with him on this assumption. If the other person knows that already, then we
have to strengthen him in the knowledge. If he does
not know it yet or no longer knows it, our business is to
transmit this knowledge to him. On the basis of the
knowledge of the humanity of God no other attitude
to any kind of fellow man is possible. It is identical with
the practical acknowledgement of his human rights and
his human dignity. To deny it to him would be for
us to renounce having Jesus Christ as Brother and God
as Father.

The distinction due to man as such through the

humanity of God, however, extends also to everything with which man as man is endowed and equipped by God, his Creator. This gift, his humanity, is not blotted out through the fall of man, nor is its goodness diminished. Man is not elected to intercourse with God because, by virtue of his humanity, he deserved such preference. He is elected through God's grace alone. He is elected, however, as the being especially endowed by God. This is manifest in his special bodily nature, in which he of course has ever so much in common with plant and animal, and also in the fact that he is a rationally thinking, willing, and speaking being destined for responsible and spontaneous decision. Above all, however, it is shown in the fact that from the beginning he is constituted, bound, and obligated as a fellow man. God concerns Himself with, loves, and calls him as *this* being in his particular totality. In bringing into action his particular nature man, as *this* being, may and should praise Him and be submissive to His grace in thankfulness. It would not do even partially to cast suspicion upon, undervalue, or speak ill of his humanity, the gift of God, which characterises him as this being. We can meet God only within the limits of humanity determined by Him. But in these limits we may meet Him. He does not reject the human! Quite the contrary! We must hold fast to this.

The distinction of man, however, goes still further. It extends itself indeed even to the particular human activity based on his endowment, to what one is accustomed to call human *culture* in its higher and lower levels. Whether as creators or as beneficiaries of culture, we all participate in it as persons responsible for it. We *can* exercise no abstinence towards it, even if we want to. But we should not *want* to do that. Each of us has his place and his function in its history. Certainly we must here consider the fact that the use of the good gift of God and hence human activity with its great and small results is compromised in the extreme through man's perverted attitude towards God, towards his neighbour, and towards himself. Certainly culture testifies clearly in history and in the present to the fact that man is *not* good but rather a downright monster. But even if one were in this respect the most melancholy sceptic, one could not—in view of the humanity of God which is bestowed upon the man who is not good or who is even monstrous—say that culture speaks only of the evil in man. What is culture in itself except the attempt of man to be man and thus to hold the good gift of his humanity in honour and to put it to work That in this attempt he ever and again runs aground and even accomplishes the opposite is a problem in itself, but one which in no way alters the fact that this attempt is inevitable. Above all, the fact remains that the *man* who, either as the creator or as the beneficiary, somehow participates in this attempt is the being who interests God. Finally, it also remains true that God, as Creator and Lord of man, is always free to produce even in human activity and its results, in spite of the problems involved, *parables* of His own eternal good will and actions. It is more than ever true, then, that with regard to these no proud abstention but only reverence, joy, and gratitude are appropriate.

We must affirm as a second consequence the fact that, through the humanity of God, a quite definite theme is given to *theological* culture in particular. Yes, along with pyramid building, pre- and post-Kantian philosophy, classical poetry, socialism, and theoretical and practical nuclear physics there is also theological culture! Since God in His deity is human, this culture must occupy itself neither with God in Himself nor with man in himself but with the man-encountering God and the God-encountering man and with their dialogue and history, in which their communion takes place and comes to its fulfilment. For this reason theology can think and speak only as it looks at Jesus Christ and from the vantage point of what He is. It cannot introduce Him. Neither can it bring about that dialogue, history, and communion. It does not have the disposition of these things. It is dependent upon the Holy Scripture, according to which the covenant is *in full effect* and in which Jesus Christ *witnesses* to *Himself*. It hears this witness. It trusts it and is satisfied with it.

Thus through all the centuries theology was, and also to-day is, given its subject-matter—its theme—and, along with this, instruction in the scholarly and practical objectivity appropriate to it. Theology must hold fast to this objectivity in its exegesis; in its investigation, presentation, and interpretation of the Christian past and present; in its dogmatics and ethics; and in its preaching, instruction, and pastoral ministry. This objectivity means that without allowing itself to be enticed into error, either towards the right or the left, theology will attempt to see, to understand, and to put into language the intercourse of God with man in which there comes about intercourse of man with God. It means that theology will deal with the word and act of the grace of God and the word and act of the human gratitude challenged, awakened, and nourished through it. The first will not be considered without the second nor the second without the first, and both will be approached in the sequence, distinction, and unity given

by the deity and thus the humanity of God. When it
stays with this theme, it is also in its most modest form
good—let us say for once " cultivated "—theology.

Whether the theological existentialism of Rudolf
Bultmann and his followers, close to which we find
ourselves here, carries us further towards this objectivity
which is indispensable to good theology remains yet to
be seen. It is not yet clear whether and in what sense a
genuine, concrete dialogue, history, and communion
between God and man is there envisioned, or whether it
is concerned merely with a repristination of the theology
of the believing individual who reflects on himself in
solitude (this time on his reality and unreality) and
explicates himself. The fact that to date neither the
people of Israel nor the Christian community appears
to have constitutive meaning for this theology causes
one concern. And what can be the meaning of the
" overcoming of the Subject-Object-Scheme," recently
proclaimed with such special enthusiasm, so long as it is
not made clear and guaranteed that this enterprise will
not once more lead to the anthropocentric myth and
call into question anew the *intercourse* between God
and man and thus the *object* of theology? Certainly
existentialism may have reminded us once again of the
elements of truth in the old school by introducing once
more the thought that one cannot speak of God without
speaking of man. It is to be hoped that it will not lead
us back into the old error that one can speak of man
without first, and very concretely, having spoken of the
living God.

A third consequence: God's humanity and the knowledge of it calls for a definite *attitude* and *alignment* of
Christian theological thinking and speaking. It can

never approach its subject matter in a vacuum, never in mere theory. Theology cannot fix upon, consider, and put into words any truths which rest on or are moved by themselves—neither an abstract truth about God nor about man nor about the intercourse between God and man. It can never verify, reflect, or report in a monologue. Incidentally, let it be said that there is no theological visual art. Since it is an event, the humanity of God does not permit itself to be fixed in an image.

In conformity with its object, the fundamental form of theology is the prayer and the sermon. It can take only the form of dialogue. Its presupposition and occasion consist in the fact that the commerce between God and man indeed concerns *all men,* in that in Him, namely, in Jesus Christ, the most personal affairs of them all are treated and the life and death of them all are decided. Hence they all must know about Him in order to define their own attitude and to participate in Him. Theology also presupposes that there are many— many too many—who *do not yet* or *no longer* or *do not* rightly know (indeed, in some way all this applies to every man) that it is necessary and imperative to proclaim to men, to call them together, and to communicate. This is your concern! Christian thinking revolves around God's Word of the covenant of peace and likewise around the man who in some way has not, or has not correctly, heard this Word, and to whom it must therefore by all means be proclaimed. And Christian speaking is both prayer to God and an address to this man.

It is *Kerygma,* the herald's call, the message which invites and summons, not to some sort of free-ranging speculation but to special reflection upon faith and obedience, in which man steps out of the mere "interest" of the spectator over into genuine participation[8] and in which he recognises his own God in the deity of Jesus Christ as well as himself in His humanity. The exegesis of form criticism has shown us that all this is in the New Testament and that it is normative both for the entire period following the resurrection of Jesus Christ and for that period preceding His direct, universal, and conclusive revelation. In the *Kerygma* man recognises himself as being under God's judgment and grace, as the receiver of His promise and His command, and thus enters with his own understanding, will, and heart into the reality of that intercourse. Theological thinking and speaking indeed cannot cause this to happen to him. Therefore it cannot have the character of address alone; it must also have the character of prayer. For that reason it can be useful to him and therefore precisely on the basis of this usefulness it must, conformably to the humanity of God Himself, be carried on. Should it not be carried out in this useful way, it would drop not only out of its role but also out of its character; it would betray itself so that, however " Christian " its content might be, it would become profane thinking and speaking.

The question of *language*, about which one must speak in reference to the so-called " outsiders," is not so burning to-day as is asserted in various quarters. This is true in the first place because, again thinking in terms of the humanity of God, we cannot at all reckon in a serious way with *real* " outsiders," with a " world come of age," but only with a world which *regards* itself as of age (and proves daily that it is precisely not that). Thus the

---

[8] Barth engages in a German-Latin play on words: man steps out of the mere " *Interesse* " . . . into genuine " *Inter-Esse.*"

so-called " outsiders " are really only " insiders " who
have not yet understood and apprehended themselves as
such. On the other hand, even the most persuaded
Christian, in the final analysis, must and will recognise
himself ever and again as an " outsider." So there must
then be no particular language for insiders and outsiders.
Both are contemporary men-of-the-world—all of us
are. A little " non-religious " language from the street,
the newspaper, literature, and, if one is ambitious, from
the philosopher may thus, for the sake of communication,
occasionally indeed be in order. However, we should not
become particularly concerned about this. A little of
the language of Canaan, a little " revelation-positivism,"
can also be a good thing in addressing us all and,
according to my experience, in which I am certainly
not alone, will often, though not always, be still better
understod even by the oddest strangers. That is better
than feeling compelled to approach them—like a " Jesuit
in miniature," certainly no sympathetic figure—with
some sort of gibberish, which, for the moment, is modern.
What we have to say to them—and first to ourselves—
is a strange piece of news—the message of the eternal
love of God directed to us men as we at all times were,
are, and shall be. Then we shall certainly be very well
understood by them, whatever they may or may not
do with it. He whose heart is really with God and
therefore really with men may have faith that the
Word of God, to which he seeks to bear witness, will
not return unto Him void.

A fourth consequence : the *sense* and *sound* of our word
must be fundamentally *positive*. Proclamation of the
covenant of God with men, announcement of the place
which is once for all opened and assigned to man in this

covenant, the message of Immanuel, the message of
Christ—this is the task. The dialogue and encounter
which are our theological theme involve God's grace and
man's gratitude. To open up again the abyss closed in
Jesus Christ cannot be our task. Man is *not* good : that
is indeed true and must once more be asserted. God does
not turn towards him without uttering in inexorable
sharpness a "No" to his transgression. Thus theology
has no choice but to put this "No" into words within
the framework of its theme. However, it must be the
"No" which Jesus Christ has taken upon Himself for
us men, in order that it may no longer affect us and
that we may no longer place ourselves under it. What
takes place in God's humanity is, since it includes that
"No" in itself, the *affirmation* of man.

The direction of our word is given therewith. The
man with whom we have to do in ourselves and in others,
although a rebel, a sluggard, a hypocrite, is likewise the
creature to whom his Creator is faithful and not unfaith-
ful. But there is still more : he is the being whom God
has loved, loves, and will love, because He has substituted
Himself in Jesus Christ and has made Himself the
guarantee. "Jesus is the victor" and "You men are
gods" : these two watchwords of Blumhardt hold good!
And with this explanation the statement that the human
spirit is naturally Christian may also be valid as an
obstinately joyful proclamation. That is what we have
to testify to men in view of the humanism *of God*,
irrespective of the more or less dense godlessness of *their*
humanism—everything else must be said only in the
framework of this statement and promise. Thus the
bitterest indictments and the most sombre threats of
judgment of the Old Testament prophets are uttered only
in the context of the history of the covenant founded by

Yahweh and faithfully preserved despite all the unfaith-
fulness of Israel. Thus the Baptist's preaching of repen-
tance had its basis and meaning only in the Kingdom
of heaven which was already at hand. Thus again
certain terrifying passages towards the end of John's
Apocalypse find their place and therewith their limits in
its final words : "Amen, come Lord Jesus! The grace
of the Lord Jesus be with all." The Word of God
announced good news to the poor, liberation to the
imprisoned, sight to the blind, justification and sanctification and even a call to service to sinners, whether gross
or refined. Consider what follows from that : to uncover
and expose misunderstandings as such is one thing;
to understand and to guide into understanding is another.
Hence, moral earnestness is a praiseworthy thing and
the gift of penetrating and perhaps witty analysis of the
times, of the situation, and of the soul is certainly a
fine gift. But the task of bringing the gospel to light is
more urgent than manifesting that earnestness and
bringing this gift into play. He to whom this *positive*
task is not absolutely the supreme task, who first of all
wants to shout at, bewilder, or laugh at men on account
of their folly and malice, had better remain silent
altogether. There is only *one* analogy to the humanity of
God in this respect, namely, the message of the great
joy—which comforts but in so doing really judges—
which is prepared for man by God and which he in
turn may have in God. "All my springs are in you!"
(Psalm 87 :7.)

Does this mean universalism? I wish here to make only
three short observations, in which one is to detect no
position for or against that which passes among us under
this term.

1. One should not surrender himself in any case to

the panic which this word seems to spread abroad, before informing himself exactly concerning its possible sense or non-sense.

2. One should at least be stimulated by the passage, Colossians 1:19, which admittedly states that God has determined through His Son as His image and as the first-born of the whole Creation to "reconcile all things (τὰ πάντα) to himself," to consider whether the concept could not perhaps have a good meaning. The same can be said of parallel passages.

3. One question should for a moment be asked, in view of the "danger" with which one may see this concept gradually surrounded. What of the "danger" of the eternally sceptical-critical theologian who is ever and again suspiciously questioning, because fundamentally always legalistic and therefore in the main morosely gloomy? Is not his presence among us currently more threatening than that of the unbecomingly cheerful indifferentism or even antinomianism, to which one with a certain understanding of universalism could in fact deliver himself? This much is certain, that we have no theological right to set any sort of limits to the loving-kindness of God which has appeared in Jesus Christ. Our theological duty is to see and understand it as being still greater than we had seen before.

And now in conclusion still a fifth consequence: in the knowledge of the humanity of God one must take seriously, affirm, and thankfully acknowledge *Christendom*, the *Church*. We must, each in his place, take part in its life and join in its service. It was a part of the exaggerations of which we were guilty in 1920 that we were able to see the theological relevance of the Church only as a negative counterpart to the Kingdom of God which

we had then so happily rediscovered. We wanted to
interpret the form of the Church's doctrine, its worship,
its juridical order as " human, all too human," as " not
so important." We regarded all the earnestness or even
zeal devoted to them as superfluous or even injurious. In
all this we at least approached the theory and practice
of a spiritual partisanship and an esoteric gnosticism.

It is now, in view of the actual and recurrent Roman
temptation, certainly not appropriate to silence or even
to soften the stress on the judgment beginning with the
house of God which, after all, runs through the entire
Bible. It is likewise inappropriate, in view of the ecclesi-
astical, confessional, and on the whole traditional—even
clerical and liturgical—restoration and reaction current
in present-day Germany, which perhaps one day may
encroach upon our land. And it certainly was and
is no good undertaking to reverse the sequence whereby
event precedes *institution*, which is also established by
the entire Bible. We had and still have to see and to
understand, however, that the maintenance of this
sequence and the remembrance of that judgment must in
no case result in neglect or renunciation of our solidarity
with the Church. The word which is critical of the
Church can be meaningful and fruitful only when it
stems from insight—I do not say too much—into the
existence and function of the Church as necessary for
salvation. It must be spoken with the intention of serving
her in her gathering together, her edification and mission.
The humanity of God is relevant to the old and the
new Israel, to the individual man who exists in his own
place and not in some sort of vacuum. Jesus Christ is
the Head of His body and only so is He also the Head
of its members. The acknowledgement of God's work
accomplished in Him implies that it has taken place

for *us* and thus only in this way for *me*. The Lord's Prayer is a *we*-prayer and only in this way also an *I*-prayer. " We " are the Church. The Church is the particular people, the congregation, or in Calvin's term, the company, which through a bit of knowledge of the gracious God manifest in Jesus Christ is constituted, appointed, and called as His witness in the world. This knowledge is paltry indeed, but because it is established by the Holy Spirit, it is unconquerable.

What is the existence of this particular people but the reflection of the humanity of God, although it is admittedly everywhere blurred and darkened and in its continuity all too often interrupted? This turning of God to man calls out and awakens some to worship, praise, and serve Him—many of them for the time being as representative of others and as His messengers to them. We should be inhuman where God is human, we should be ashamed of the Church. What Jesus Christ is for God and for us, on earth and in time, He is as Lord of this community, as King of this people, as Head of this body and of all its members. He is all these with and in this inconspicuous, painfully divided, and otherwise very questionable Christendom. He is all these with, among, and in the Christians whom one can admire or even love only in the face of many serious difficulties. He is all these as the Reconciler and Redeemer of the whole world. He is all these, however, in the strange communion of these strange saints. The Church is not too mean a thing for Him but, for better or for worse, sufficiently precious and worthy in His eyes to be entrusted with His witnessing and thus His affairs in the world—yes, even Himself. So great is God's loving-kindness !

For this reason there is no private Christianity. For this reason we cannot but take seriously, affirm, and love this community in its peculiarity. While we cannot but view critically in all details its assuredly human—all too human—efforts for better knowledge and better confession, for its meetings, its inner order, and its outward task, we must also view them as seriously important. For this reason, too, theology cannot be carried on in the private lighthouses of some sort of merely personal discoveries and opinions. It can be carried on only in the Church—it can be put to work in all its elements only in the context of the questioning and answering of the Christian community and in the rigorous service of its commission to all men. One must perhaps himself have had a part in the life of the Church during a difficult period to know that there are hours in its work, its struggle, and its suffering in which not less than everything can depend upon some human, very human, iota or dot in its decisions and also in its thinking and speaking. One will then approach more cautiously the mood in which one sees only inconsequential matters in the Church. In a really living Church there is perhaps nothing inconsequential at all.

But however that may be, our "I believe in the Holy Spirit" would be empty if it did not also include in a concrete, practical, and obligatory way the "I believe one Holy Catholic and Apostolic Church." We believe the Church as the place where the crown of humanity, namely, man's fellow-humanity, may become visible in Christocratic brotherhood. Moreover, we believe it as the place where God's glory wills to dwell upon earth, that is, where humanity—the humanity of God—wills to assume tangible form in time and here upon earth.

Here we recognise the humanity of God. Here we delight in it. Here we celebrate and witness to it. Here we glory in the Immanuel, just as He did who, as He looked at the world, would not cast away the burden of the Church but rather chose to take it upon Himself and bear it in the name of all its members. " If God is for us, who is against us?"

THE GIFT OF FREEDOM[1]

Foundation of Evangelical Ethics

It is my task to discuss the gift of freedom, and to do so with the foundation of evangelical ethics in view. Let me anticipate the solution to the problem inherent in this theme in three summary propositions. The first describes the freedom which *God* Himself possesses; the second delineates it as the gift bestowed by God upon *man*; the third relates the consequences of these two to the problem of the foundation of evangelical *ethics*.

First: *God's freedom is His very own.* It is the sovereign grace wherein God chooses to commit Himself to man. Thereby God is Lord as *man's* God.

Secondly: *Man's freedom is his as the gift of God.* It is the joy wherein man appropriates God's election. Thereby man is God's creature, His partner, and His child as *God's* man.

Thirdly: Evangelical ethics is the reflection upon the *divine call to human action* which is implied by the gift of freedom.

I

We begin by examining what man may know about *God's own freedom.* Must I justify my starting with God's own freedom rather than with anything else?

[1] This address, translated by Thomas Weiser, was given at a meeting of the *Gesellschaft für evangelische Theologie*, Bielefeld, 21st September, 1953.

Must I justify my not beginning with man's innate or given freedom? I, too, have heard the news that we can speak about *God* only by speaking about *man*. I do not contest this claim. Rightly interpreted, it may be an expression of the true insight that God is not without man. This means in our particular context that God's own freedom must be recognised as freedom to be a partisan for man.

We may not speak of God's own freedom apart from the history of God's dealings with man. Man's God-given freedom, then, must be acknowledged from the very beginning. But this claim, correctly understood, calls for a counterclaim. We can speak about man only by speaking about God. This general statement is hardly disputed among Christian theologians. There is, however, sharp disagreement as to the priority of the two claims. It is my firm conviction that what I have just called the counterclaim is the true claim and must come first. Why deny priority to God in the realm of knowing when it is uncontested in the realm of being? If God is the first reality, how can man be the first truth?

Those holding the opposite view go so far as to say that the God-given freedom of man is, first of all, freedom of man from himself. But how does this bold statement prompt man to begin as a thinker with himself as a starting point? Why, of all concepts in Christian theology, should the concept of God merely have the function of a boundary term? Why should it connote only a vacuum to be filled at best with subsequent and nonessential assertions about the ideal or historical conditions of human existence? Is it so self-evident that man is intimately known to us, whereas God remains the great and doubtful Unknown? Is it, then, a law of the Medes and the Persians that our quest for God must proceed on the basis of our supposed knowledge of man? Does not this freedom, bestowed by God upon man and, as we shall discuss later, specifically upon the Christian theologian, prompt man to overcome this mental block and to think in a new perspective, to think even exclusively in a new perspective? Is not this new perspective mapped out for man in God's revelation, showing forth first and foremost God Himself, and in this way and only then revealing man to himself? Where else can we learn that freedom exists and what it is, except in confrontation with God's own freedom offered to us as the source and measure of all freedom? We do not speculate beyond man nor do we abandon him and his freedom by first inquiring about the One who is man's *God* and about His own freedom. On the contrary, we then may seek and find true man and his true freedom.

God's freedom is not merely unlimited possibility or formal majesty and omnipotence, that is to say empty, naked sovereignty. Nor is this true of the God-given freedom of man. If we so misinterpret human freedom, it irreconcilably clashes with divine freedom and becomes the false freedom of sin, reducing man to a prisoner. God Himself, if conceived of as unconditioned power, would be a demon and as such His own prisoner. In the light of His revelation, God is free in word and deed; He is the source and measure of all freedom, insofar as He is the Lord, choosing and determining Himself first of all. In His own freedom, as the source of human freedom, God above all willed and determined Himself to be the Father and the Son in the unity of the Spirit. This is not abstract freedom. Nor is it the freedom of aloof isolation. Likewise, man's God-given freedom is not to be sought and found in any solitary detachment from God. In God's own freedom there is encounter and communion; there is order and, consequently, dominion and subordination; there is majesty and humility, absolute authority and absolute obedience; there is offer and response.

God's freedom is the freedom of the Father and the Son in the unity of the Spirit. Again, man's freedom is a far cry from the self-assertion of one or many solitary individuals. It has nothing to do with division and disorder. God's own freedom is trinitarian, embracing grace, thankfulness, and peace. It is the freedom of the living God. Only in this relational freedom is God sovereign, almighty, the Lord of all.

In this freedom God is, again according to His revelation, *man's* God. To put it more concretely : He is the God of Abraham, Isaac, and Jacob. He is man's God not because man projected, patterned, and exalted Him, not because Israel chose Him, but because He chose, decided, and determined Himself for His Israel and with Israel for mankind. The well-known definitions of the essence of God and in particular of His freedom, containing such terms as " wholly other," " transcendence," or "non-worldly," stand in need of thorough clarification if fatal misconceptions of human freedom as well are to be avoided. The above definitions might just as well fit a dead idol. Negative as they are, they most certainly miss the very centre of the Christian concept of God, the radiant affirmation of free grace, whereby God bound and committed Himself to man, making Himself in His Son a man of Israel and the brother of all men, appropriating human nature into the unity of His own being. If this is true, if this is not an accidental historical fact but in its historical uniqueness is the revelation of the divine will, valid and powerful before, above, after, and in all history, then God's freedom is essentially not freedom *from*, but freedom *to* and *for*. (We shall have to remember this point in our discussion of human freedom.) God is free for *man*, free to coexist with man and, as the Lord of the covenant, to participate in his *history*. The concept of God without man is indeed as anomalous as wooden iron.

In His free grace, God is for man in every respect; He surrounds man from all sides. He is man's Lord who is before him, above him, after him, and thence also with him in history, the locus of man's existence. Despite man's insignificance, God is with him as his Creator who intended and made mankind to be very good. Despite man's sin, God is with him, the One who was in Jesus Christ reconciling the world, drawing man unto Himself in merciful judgment. Man's evil past is not merely crossed out because of its irrelevancy. Rather, it is in the good care of God. Despite man's life in the flesh, corrupt and ephemeral, God is with him. The victor in Christ is here and now present through His Spirit, man's strength, companion, and comfort. Despite man's death God is with him, meeting him as redeemer and perfecter at the threshold of the future to show him the totality of existence in the true light in which the eyes of God beheld it from the beginning and will behold it evermore. In what He is for man and does for man, God ushers in the history leading to the ultimate salvation of man.

Though in a different way, God is beyond doubt also before, above, after, and with all of His other creatures. However, we may at best venture some ideas of this difference in the meaning of God's freedom for these creatures, of the gift of freedom to them. In reality we have no precise knowledge about this.

Through His revelation God is known in His loving-kindness to us as the God of *man*. However, God was not and is not bound to choose and to decide Himself for man alone and to show His loving-kindness to him alone. The thought of any insignificant being outside the human cosmos being far more worthy of divine attention than man is deeply edifying and should not be lightly dismissed. But it remains true that God who gave His Son to become and to remain our brother assures us that He willed to love *man*, that He loved us and still loves us and shall love us because He chose and determined Himself to be our God.

This freedom of God as it is expressed in His being, word, and deed is the content of the *Gospel*. Receiving this good news from those who witness to it, the Christian *community* in the world is called to acknowledge it in faith, to respond to it in love, to set on it its hope and trust, and to proclaim it to the world which belongs to this free God. It is the privilege and the mission of the Christian community to acknowledge and to confess the Gospel. By acknowledging and confessing Jesus Christ as the creation and revelation of God's freedom, this community is incorporated into the body of Christ and becomes the earthly and historical form of His existence. He is in its midst.

We do well to keep remembering that the existence of the Christian community, through its preaching and its works, is already an expression of man's God-given freedom. Let us therefore respect the difference in perspective! The existence of the Christian community in its faith, love, and hope, and in its proclamation, is unmistakably part of the divinely inaugurated *Heilsgeschichte*. It is part of it insofar as to acknowledge and confess God's freedom is an act of freedom bestowed

upon man in the course of this history. But it is and
remains an act of human freedom. The divine freedom
was not initiated in and by this act of human freedom.
Nor is it accomplished and somehow encompassed in
it. Rather, God's freedom is and remains above and
beyond human freedom. Measured against the act of
divine freedom, the act of human freedom has its own
beginning, its own course, and its own preliminary and
relative ends. None of these coincide or are to be con-
founded with those of the *Heilsgeschichte*. It remains
the prerogative of the divine freedom to set the end of
this history, the beginning of which it set also.

God's own freedom and its realisations is the source
and object of every Christian act of recognition and
confession. It is sufficient that this human act takes
place in the context of the freedom of God to which
it bears witness. Yahweh lives and will live in solidarity,
but not in identity, with Israel. The same holds true
for Jesus Christ, the word and deed of God, with regard
to His community, to the task it has to perform in
response to the gift of freedom, and to its *kerygma*.
The head does not become the body and the body does
not become the head. The king does not become his
own messenger, and the messenger does not become
king. It is sufficient that the community be called into
being, be created, protected, and sustained by Jesus
Christ, and that it may confess Him who came into
the world, is present now, and shall come in glory. It
may confess Him who was, is, and shall be the word
and deed of God's freedom and of His all-embracing
loving-kindness.

II

God in His own freedom bestows human freedom. Here we must point to so-called *natural* freedom which constitutes and characterises human existence in its creatureliness, and to the freedom of eternal life *promised* to man. Here, for once, we must daringly include both in what is to be said about *Christian* freedom. Christian freedom is divinely bestowed upon man despite his sin, despite his existence in the flesh, and despite his being threatened by death. " Natural freedom " and " freedom promised " must, in any event, be understood on the basis of " Christian freedom." This is because freedom is made known to us by God as the " freedom of the Christian man."

Human freedom is the *gift* of God in the free out-pouring of His grace. To call a man free is to recognise that God has *given* him freedom. Human freedom is enacted within history, that history which leads to the ultimate salvation of man. Human freedom never ceases to be the event wherein the free God gives and man receives this gift. God freely makes Himself available to man by granting him the freedom he is meant to have. Whatever the subsequent events of this history may be, they take place within the context and under the judgment of this divine act of mercy. Seen from the vantage point of the free gift of the free God, the concept of unfree man is a contradiction in itself. Unfree man is a creature of chaos, a monster begotten by his own pride, his own laziness, his own lies.

The concept of freedom as man's rightful claim and due is equally contradictory and impossible. So is the thought of man's acquiring freedom by earning it or buying it at any price. The idea that man can conquer freedom as God's antagonist and defiantly wrench it from Him is untenable. Man has no real will power. Nor does he get it by himself. His power lies in receiving and in appropriating God's gift. The event of man's freedom is the event of his thankfulness for the gift, of his sense of responsibility as a receiver, of his loving care for what is given him. It is his reverence before the free God who accepts him as His partner without relinquishing His sovereignty. This event alone is the event of freedom.

The gift of freedom, however, involves more than being offered one option among several. It involves more than being asked a question, being presented with an opportunity, and having a possibility opened up. The gift of freedom is total, unequivocal, and irrevocable. It remains the gift of freedom even though it may be turned into man's judgment if misunderstood or misused. We are dealing with the gift of the free God. God does not put man into the situation of Hercules at the crossroads. The opposite is true. God frees man from this false situation. He lifts him from appearance to reality. It is true that man's God-given freedom is choice, decision, act. But it is genuine choice; it is genuine decision and act in the right direction.

It would be a strange freedom that would leave man neutral, able equally to choose, decide, and act rightly or wrongly! What kind of power would that be! Man becomes free and is free by choosing, deciding, and determining himself in accordance with the freedom of God. The source of man's freedom is also its yardstick. Trying to escape from being in accord with God's own freedom is not human freedom. Rather, it is a compulsion wrought by powers of darkness or by man's own helplessness. Sin as an alternative is not anticipated or included in the freedom given to man by God. Nor can sin be explained and theoretically justified by this freedom. No excuse can be provided for sin. In human freedom there is no room for sin by fiat. Sinful man is not free, he is a captive, a slave. When genuine human freedom is realised, inevitably the door to the " right " opens and the door to the " left " is shut. This inevitability is what makes God's gift of freedom so marvellous, and yet at the same time so terrifying.

As a gift of God, human freedom cannot contradict divine freedom. This leads to certain limitations regarding human freedom which are similar to those mentioned in our earlier attempts to define the freedom of God. We now make bold to say:

(1) Human freedom as a gift of God does not allow for any vague choices between various possibilities. The reign of chance and ambiguity is excluded. For the free God Himself, the giver of man's freedom, is no blind accident, no tyrant. He is the Lord, choosing and determining Himself unmistakably once and for all. He is His own law.

(2) Human freedom is not realised in the solitary detachment of an individual in isolation from his fellow men. God is *a se* (for Himself), but He is *pro nobis* (for us). For us! It is true that He who gave man freedom because He is man's friend, is also *pro me* (for me). But I am not Man, I am only *a man*, and I am a man only in relation to my fellow men. Only in encounter and in communion with them may I receive the gift of freedom. God is *pro me* because He is *pro nobis*.

(3) Human freedom is only secondarily freedom *from* limitations and threats. Primarily it is freedom *for*.

(4) Human freedom is not to be understood as freedom to assert, to preserve, to justify and save oneself. God is primarily free *for*; the Father is free for the Son, the Son for the Father in the unity of the Spirit. The one God is free for man as his Creator, as the Lord of the covenant, as the beginner and perfecter of his history, his *Heilsgeschichte*. God says "Yes." Only once this "Yes" is said, He also says "No." Thereby He reveals Himself to be *free from* all that is alien and hostile to His nature. Only once this "Yes" is said, is He free for Himself and for His own glory. Human freedom is freedom only within the limitations of God's own freedom.

And thus we can see that freedom is *being joyful*. Freedom is the great gift, totally unmerited and wondrous beyond understanding. It awakens the receiver to true selfhood and new life. It is a gift from *God*, from the source of all goodness, an ever-new token of His faithfulness and mercy. The gift is unambiguous and cannot fail. Through this gift man who was irretrievably separated and alienated from God is called into discipleship. This is why freedom is joy! Certainly, man does not live up to this freedom. Even worse, he fails in every respect. It is true enough that he does not know any longer the natural freedom which was bestowed upon him in creation; he does not know as yet the ultimate freedom in store for him at the completion of his journey, in the ultimate fulfilment of his existence. It is true enough that man may presently know and enjoy this freedom through the abiding Spirit of the Father and the Son only in spite of sin, flesh, and death; in spite of the world, his earthly anxiety and his worldly nature; and in spite of himself in his persistent temptation. This however, does not prevent man from being enabled to know and to live out this freedom in incomparable and inexhaustible joy, limited as his own awareness may be. Some may not want any part of it, and at times we all feel this way. But this does not change anything. God's gift is there for all. It is poured out at the beginning of our journey, at its destination, and most certainly also in our present plight. Freedom is waiting here and now to be received and lived out in joy, albeit a joy that is not without travail.

Human freedom is the joy whereby man appropriates for himself God's election. God has elected Himself in His Son to be the God, Lord, Shepherd, Saviour, and Redeemer of mankind. Through His own election, He willed man to be His creature, His partner, and His son, He, the God of the community of men, and we, the community of men, His people! Freedom is the joy whereby man acknowledges and confesses this divine election by willing, deciding, and determining himself to be the echo and mirror of the divine act. Each individual is called to this commitment in the midst of the community of men, not as the first disciple but as a follower in the visible and invisible footsteps of many; not as the only one but together with many known and unknown fellow Christians. He may be accompanied by the comforting help of several or by at least a few. He may be a rather sad member of the rear guard or he may be way ahead of the crowd where he is temporarily alone. He lives for himself, but not only for himself. He is constantly in living relationship to others, as a member of the people of God who appropriates for himself God's election and is responsible for the brothers. Each individual is called by his own name as a member of the people of God. Each one is responsible for his relationship with God and his fellow men. He is free because he chooses, decides, and determines himself to be this person. His freedom is the joy of that obedience which is given to him. This is a daring venture whenever it is undertaken. A venture at one's own risk and peril? Never! It is the venture of responsibility in the presence of the Giver and the fellow receivers of the gift —past, present, and future. It is the venture of obedience whereby man reflects in his own life God's offer and his own response. This is the life of obedience, allowed for by man's freedom : to will himself to be that member of God's household which God willed him to be.

Free man wills himself to be God's *creature* according to that distinctive structure and limitation of his human nature which sets man apart from all other beings. God wants man free together with his fellow men in the greatness and the misery, in the promise and the anxiety, in the richness and the poverty of his humanity. True enough, man no longer knows what it means to be truly human. Alienated from God, he is alienated from himself and from his true nature. But God does not cease to call and to claim this estranged creature for His own. Likewise, man does not cease to be called and claimed by God as this estranged creature. The gift of freedom makes man free to be not more and not less than human. Whatever God's other intentions for man may be, they will always be a confirmation of his nature as a creature of God. And whatever man may choose to do with his God-given freedom, it always will have to be carried out within the framework of human possibilities. If he cannot boast of his human condition and achievement because they are a gift of God, he need not be ashamed of them either. God does not expect extraordinary accomplishments nor does he expect a jaded or lazy response. He does, however, expect man to realise in his life the divine intention of true humanity inherent in the gift. Glorifying God and loving his neighbour are sure signs of man's commitment.

God wants man to be His creature. Furthermore, He wants him to be His *partner*. There is a *causa Dei* in the world. God wants light, not darkness. He wants cosmos, not chaos. He wants peace, not disorder. He wants man to administer and to receive justice rather than to inflict and to suffer injustice. He wants man to live according to the Spirit rather than according to the flesh. He wants man bound and pledged to Him rather than to any other authority. He wants man to live and not to die. Because He wills these things God is Lord, Shepherd, and Redeemer of man, who in His holiness and mercy meets His creature; who judges and forgives, rejects and receives, condemns and saves. This is not the place to describe the divine act of reconciliation even in its main outline. It is enough to say that God's "Yes" and "No," spoken in His act of reconciliation, is not proclaimed apart from man. Even in this central act God declines to be alone, without man. God insists on man's participation in His reconciling work. He wants man, not as a secondary God, to be sure, but as a truly free follower and co-worker, to repeat His divine "Yes" and "No." This is the meaning of God's covenant with man. This is the task man is called to fulfil when God enters into the covenant relationship with him. This is the freedom of discipleship bestowed upon him.

The sovereign God alone saved man from the alienation and depravity of which he was and still is guilty. He delivered him from the imprisonment and slavery which was and still is his human lot. In the death of Jesus Christ, perfect reconciliation, beyond any need for improvement or repetition, took place once and for all. In His resurrection, and nowhere else, as long as time lasts, God's act of reconciliation is unmistakably revealed. There is no need whatsoever for this divine act to be re-enacted by man in order to be efficacious. This is not to say, however, that man is confined to the role of an approving spectator. The gift of freedom becomes operative at this critical point. Man's freedom always remains human freedom and is not to be confused with the divine freedom whereby God in Jesus Christ took man's part.

Human freedom is the God-given freedom to obey. *Faith* is the obedience of the *pilgrim* who has his vision and his trust set upon God's free act of reconciliation. This obedience confirms and evinces the transition from sin to righteousness, from the flesh to the spirit, from the law to the sovereignty of the living God, from death to life in the small and preliminary, yet determined, steps of the daily journey. *Love* is the obedience of the *witness* who is summoned to announce this transition. The witness announces God's victorious deed, offered to all his brothers and sisters far and nigh so that they might greet it as their light. This obedience in love and faith is the human response to the divine offer of justification, sanctification, and calling in Jesus Christ.

Thus human freedom is freedom to respond with thanksgiving. It is the *freedom of the Christian man* whom God chooses to be His partner and whom He does not abandon. God does not expect from man more than this gratitude, this faith, and this love. Nor does He expect less, and He certainly expects nothing else! For this service of thankful obedience, for this participation in the *causa Dei*, God has set man free.

God wants man to be His creature and His partner.

Even more, He wants him to be His *child*. God is not content with man living as a reverent creature *before* Him, or as a grateful partner *alongside* Him. He wants him to be a man *with* Him, and to enjoy the glorious assurance of belonging to God. This assurance points to man's future, his eternal life. But man as he is here and now, cannot see himself enjoying this eternal relationship. He cannot understand himself in this dimension, not even in faith and love. Man bestowed with eternal life is future man; he is the object of God's promise and of our hope. And yet he is not devoid of reality. In God's free deed, in Jesus Christ, man *is* God's child. But as long as man lives he remains a pilgrim and a witness. He can only call on God from afar and out of the depth, *" Our Father who art in heaven!"* He does not yet understand himself as the child who enjoys the glorious assurance of belonging to the Father. For as yet he is an enigma to himself, and his brothers and sisters in the Christian community are enigmas to him as well. As yet his eternal destination is hidden and not revealed.

Even though man as he is here and now does not see or understand himself as a child of God, the God-given freedom breaks through in a new dimension, in a decisive and definitive way. Man is free to call God " Our Father," here and now. Man is free to see things from the standpoint of the beginning, the revealed act of the free God in the here and now. He can see his end in the ultimate revelation of God's act, his belonging to Him in glory. Frustrated, yet comforted in the midst of frustration, he will steadfastly look to the end. Human freedom is to live, to suffer, and finally to die in this expectation. But before he dies, as long as the day lasts, man is free to work, to rise after each fall, to labour and not to grow weary. Whether or not we rise or tire depends on the use we make of our freedom to look to the end. " Jesus, give me eyes, and touch my eyes that they may serve,"[2] says a well-known hymn. Man is free to bring his plea before God. In so doing he is free to hope for the great light, the great vision that will illumine the world, the Church, his fellow man, and himself. A Christian is one who makes use of this freedom to pray and to live in the hope of the end which will be the revelation of the beginning.

III

We now turn to the question of what these assumptions may teach us about the foundation of *evangelical ethics*. Although we cannot elaborate on these foundations at this point, we can at least give an outline.[3]

A free man is one who chooses, decides, and determines himself and who acts according to his thoughts, words, and deeds. The course of his actions is a consequence of the nature of his God-given freedom. It is therefore in order to use interchangeably freedom and commandment. Man does the good when he acts according to the imperative inherent in the gift of freedom. He does the evil when he obeys a law that is contrary to his freedom. But these definitions need to be qualified.

Man's freedom as the directive and criterion for his actions is the gift bestowed upon him in a historical event of the free God's encounter with him. The giver

[2] " Jesus, gib gesunde Augen, die was taugen, rühre meine Augen an."
[3] Those interested in a more detailed description may consult *Church Dogmatics*, I, 2 (par. 22, sec. 3) II, 2 (par. 36-39), III, 4.

does not retreat behind his gift, nor the lawmaker behind the law, nor divine freedom behind human freedom. It is God who determines how human freedom becomes directive and criterion for human action. Free man is subject to God's most concrete command, for through this command human freedom takes on authoritative form and the imperative whereby man is confronted and measured becomes decisive. God is always man's Creator, Reconciler, and Redeemer. He wants man to be His creature, His partner, and His child. What this means for each of us here and there, to-day and to-morrow, is decided by the free word of the free Lord in ever-renewed encounter between God and an individual. Measured against the divine commandment, man's action—his ethos—is found either good or evil. If our interpretation of divine and human freedom is accepted, these terms affirm the content and consequence of the imperative and the criterion, and concurrently exclude any arbitrary and accidental characteristics.

Ethics must be understood as the attempt, scientific or otherwise, to cope with the question of good and evil in human behaviour.

Ethics according to our assumption can only be *evangelical ethics*. The question of good and evil is never answered by man's pointing to the authoritative Word of God in terms of a set of rules. It is never discovered by man or imposed on the self and others as a code of good and evil actions, a sort of yardstick of what is good and evil. Holy Scripture defies being forced into a set of rules; it is a mistake to use it as such. The ethicist cannot take the place either of the free God or of free man, even less of both together. His prescriptions in no way prejudge either the divine imperative or human obedience. On what authority would he prescribe, even though he quoted Bible verses, what a certain human being at a certain time should do or not do? Any such pretence, though well intended, is bound to lead astray. When the divine imperative urges upon man here and now a decision on a course of action, in harmony with the will of God, the ethicist will fail man with even his most realistic prescriptions and leave him utterly alone. Alas, he will be left alone not with God, but rather with himself, with his own conscience, with the *kairos*, or with his own judgment. In this realistic situation the choice between good and evil is made. To offer ethical norms to man in this predicament is to hold out a stone instead of bread.

If only ethics could reveal to man from the very beginning that in wrestling with the problem of his good or evil actions he is not confronted with his conscience, with the *kairos*, with his own judgment, with any visible or invisible law of nature or history, with any individual or social ideals, and, least of all, with his own arbitrary will. If only ethics could tell him that as a free man he is confronted with the will, word, and deed of the free God.

Ethics is a *theory* of human behaviour. This does not speak against the necessary ethical task. It merely emphasises that the ethical theory is not meant to provide man with a programme the implementation of which would be his life's goal. Nor is it meant to present man with principles to be interpreted, applied, and put into practice. Ethics has to make clear that every single step man takes involves a specific and direct responsibility towards God, who reached out for man in specific and direct encounter. This responsibility is lived out in obedience or disobedience, in good or

evil, in confirmation or in negation and loss of the gift
of freedom. Ethics exists to remind man of his confrontation with God, who is the light illuminating all his
actions. It must be man's guide in his discernment of the
apparently unlimited possibilities and in his choice of
the only true one, existing either now or in the future.
It must be man's teacher of evangelical ethics as the
ethics of free grace.

Evangelical ethics will leave the pronouncement of
unconditional imperatives to God. Its task is to emphasise the reality and the conditioning of human life,
lived in the light of the divine imperative. This does
not exclude the possibility of conditional imperatives
addressed in concrete situations by a person to a brother.
It is part of the risk of obedience involved in the
encounter and communion between Christian brothers,
and it is part of the risk of action according to the
God-given freedom, to be called to invite, even to
urge, a brother to a concrete action in a concrete
situation, and to ask from him a concrete decision. Man
will do so with his eyes lifted up to the living God who is
also his brother's God. He will do so with his mind set
on human freedom given to his brother also. If his
courage is nourished by humility before God and his
fellow men, this attitude alone may justify such conditional advice. He who takes the risk of counselling
must be prepared to be counselled in turn by his brother
if there is need of it. Such mutual counselling in a
concrete situation is an event. It is part of the ethos
which is realised ethics. It is only indirectly or not
at all a part of ethics proper. For ethics is theory and
not practice, though it is the theory about practice.
Its main problem is precisely the question of the ethos,
of the right and wrong, in human action. The ethos

of the ethicist implies that he refrain from attempting too much and becoming thereby a lawmaker.

Ethics is reflection upon what man is required to do in and with the gift of freedom. The ethicist should not want to attempt too little either. He must want to realise his calling and his talents. It is not enough to insist that human life is to be lived under the divine imperative. Ethical reflection must go further and ask the question to what extent this is so. Neither the freedom of God's commandment nor that of man's obedience is empty form. Human action takes place at the point of contact between these two spheres of freedom. Each of these is characterised by its own content, tone, and extent. Ethical reflection has to concentrate upon these. It has to begin with the recognition that the free God is the free man's Lord, Creator, Reconciler, and Redeemer, and that free man is God's creature, partner, and child. This insight will be gained at the very source of Christian thinking, in Holy Scripture, where ethical reflection will also renew, sharpen, and correct its findings in continuous searching. In addition, ethical reflection may and must consult the Christian community in its past and present history. It must do this in order to be admonished, nourished, enriched, perhaps stirred and warned, by the use which the fathers and also brethren made and still are making of Christian freedom.

Therefore, ethics is not without signposts in its attempt to point to God's authoritative word of judgment. If it is based on the knowledge of God and of man, it will receive its contour. It will not point to a vacuum, but to the true God, the real man, and the real encounter between them. The ethical quest is and remains a quest and yet is not totally devoid of fulfilment. Indirect as it may be, the quest is a witness to God's concrete

word. Ethical reflection may and must be genuine
search and genuine doctrine, genuine because true ethics
does not deprive God, its object, of His due power and
glory. It leaves the uttering of the essential and final
word to God Himself. But it does not shrink away
from the preliminary words which are necessary to
focus man's wandering thoughts on the one centre where
he, himself free, shall hear the word of the free God,
the commandment addressed to him, the judgment falling
upon him, and the promise waiting for him.

IV

These short and general comments on the foundation
of evangelical ethics may suffice. Our discussion after-
wards might well centre on the above remarks, so as
not to get sidetracked from the central theme by the
additional, and perhaps distracting, remarks I would
now like to make. Indeed, before concluding, I propose a
short excursion into the field of ethics proper, of what
we call "special ethics." I shall take as my starting
point the above-described presuppositions. We are
gathered here under the auspices of the "Gesellschaft
für evangelische Theologie" (Society for Evangelical
Theology). This is why I shall choose, as an example
and merely as an example, a small and often neglected
area : the ethics of theology itself and the ethos of the
free theologian.

Is not the free theologian also a man and as such a
recipient of the gift of freedom? Does not God address
him, his thinking, speaking, and acting as well, when
He gives man His commandment in and with the gift of
freedom? Let it be noted that according to truly evan-

gelical teaching the term "theologian" is not confined to the seminary professor, to the theological student, or to the minister. It is meant for every Christian who is mindful of the theological task entrusted to the whole Christian congregation, and who is willing and able to share in the common endeavour according to his own talents. We are about to call it a day and are rather tired. I may, therefore, be excused for substituting some isolated remarks for a systematic development of the problem. And because I belong to the old guard to-day, I may be allowed to switch, at least in feeling tone, from ethics to a sort of admonition. You may be assured that there will be no deviations into imperatives of any kind.

(1) A free theologian, free according to our definition, will be found ready, willing, and able always to begin his thinking *at the beginning*. This means his recognition of the resurrection of Jesus Christ as the directive for his reasoning. In his reflections and statements he will always first proceed from God's relationship to man and only then continue with man's relationship to God. There is an abundance of serious, pious, learned, and ingenious theological undertaking. But lacking the sky-light and hence serenity, the theologian remains a gloomy visitor upon this earth of darkness, an unpleasant instructor of his brethren, whose teachings, at best, compare with the sombre music of Beethoven and Brahms! The thoughtful theologian who refuses to begin with God is bound to begin with misery, individual and corporate, with the chaos which threatens him and the world around him, with anxieties and problems. He will turn around in circles and end up precisely where he started. Cut off from the fresh air, he considers it to be his bounden duty not to let others breathe fresh air either. Only the radical turnabout we have been

advocating here could rescue him. Nobody has accomplished this turnabout once and forever. Man has been set free for this very event, this act of obedience which calls for repetition every day, every hour, whenever a new theological task presents itself. There is no reason for complaint about the impossibility of such a turnabout. True, this turnabout is not a dialectical trick to be learned and then used merrily again and again. Without the invocation, " Our Father, who art in heaven " this turnabout cannot take place. This is why it is imperative to recognise the essence of theology as lying in the liturgical action of adoration, thanksgiving, and petition. The old saying, *Lex orandi lex credendi*, far from being a pious statement, is one of the most profound descriptions of the theological method. We cannot do without this turnabout. The free and true theologian lives from it. In the invocation, in the giving of thanks, and in the petition, this turnabout is realised and the theologian is allowed to live out the freedom of thought which he enjoys as a child of God.

(2) A free theologian starts steadily and happily with the *Bible*. Here must be his starting point, but not because any old or new orthodoxy knocked it into him; it is not a law but a privilege to start with the Bible. It is his starting point not because he abstains from reading and appreciating other godly and worldly books —not to forget the newspapers. He starts with the Bible because in the Bible he learns about the free God and free man, and as a disciple of the Bible he may himself become a witness to the divine and human freedom. He does not start with a doctrine of the canon and of the verbal inspiration of Holy Scripture. But he does begin, not without inspiration, with daily searching of canonical writings. They informed and

still inform him. He listens to them. He studies them in many ways, not despising the analytical, the historical-critical method, in order to gain a better understanding.

There are two reasons why the analysis, including the so-called " ascertained results " of historical-critical research, or the so-called "exegetical findings," is not the starting point of a free theologian. First, these results have a tendency to change every thirty years and from one exegete to another, and are thereby disqualified as a valid starting point. Secondly, analysis of both Biblical and secular texts, even though a *conditio sine qua non* of attentive listening to their message, does in no way guarantee and presuppose this act of listening. We listen when we read and study synthetically. The free theologian combines in one single act analysis and synthesis in his reading and studies. This is meditation, the secret of which is, again, adoration. The free theologian, taking the Bible as his starting point, is led by the testimony of the Bible, or more precisely by the origin, object, and content of this testimony. Here Christ spoke to him, and he let Him speak, through the medium of this testimony. Does this imply his speaking in direct quotation and interpretation of Biblical texts and contexts? Maybe often, maybe not always. The freedom bestowed upon him by the origin, object, and content of the Biblical testimony can and must be asserted through his attempt to think and to relate in his own terms what he heard in the Bible. As an illustration I refrained in this address from using one single direct quotation from the Scriptures, with the exception of the Lord's prayer at the beginning. It is only right to exercise this freedom earnestly and repeatedly. It is an excellent yardstick for our knowing what we say when we quote and interpret. In regard to church practice we may ask whether this attempt should not be made consistently in sermons, as contrasted to Bible study. The freedom of theology is both freedom for exegesis and freedom for what we call dogmatics. At least in his endeavour to sum up the content of a book of the Bible or even the variety of Biblical testimonies, the exegete embarks upon dogmatical thinking. Dogmatics is the conscious and systematic account of the common understanding of all Biblical testimonies with due regard for their variety. Only through a formidable misunderstanding can the two functions of theology— exegesis and dogmatics—be set one against the other.

(3) A free theologian does not deny, nor is he ashamed of, his indebtedness to a particular *philosophy* or ontology, to ways of thought and speech. These may be traditional or a bit original, old or new, coherent or incoherent. No one speaks exclusively in Biblical terms. As least the combination of these terms, if not the meaning they assume in his mind and in his mouth, are, willingly or not, of his own making. The Biblical authors themselves, incidentally, far from speaking a celestial language, spoke in many earthly languages. This is why a free theologian, who is not even a prophet or an apostle, will certainly not wish to dissociate himself from his brethren in Church and world by his claim to speak " as from heaven," " according to the gospel," or, if this is synonymous for him, " according to Luther." If he does speak with any such authority, his listeners must sense it without his explicit affirmation. To speak God's word must be an event and not the object of his assertion. Even then he speaks from within his philosophical shell, speaks in his own cumbersome vernacular which is certainly not identical with the tongues of angels, although the angels may utilise him at times.

Three characteristics distinguish the free from the unfree theologian. First, he is aware of his condition. Secondly, he stands ready to submit the coherence of his concepts and formulations to the coherence of the divine revelation and not conversely. Thirdly, to mention the inevitable slogan, he is a philosopher " as though he were not," and he has his ontology " as though he had it not." A free theologian will not be hindered by traditional conceptions from thinking and speaking in the direction from God to man, as affirmed at the outset of this address. His ontology will be subject to criticism and control by his theology, and not conversely. He will not necessarily feel obligated to the philosophical *kairos*, the latest prevailing philosophy. The gratitude of the Royal House of Austria will, in any event, not be showered upon him. And who knows, he may be quite glad to resort at times to an older philosophy, like the ill-famed " Subject-Object-Scheme." If we visualise for a moment the ideal situation of the free theologian, we may foresee the possibility not of theology recognising itself in any form of philosophy, but of free philosophy recognising itself in free theology. Yet the free theologian knows very well that, like a poor wretch, he does not live in this ideal situation.

(4) A free theologian thinks and speaks within the *Church*, within the communion of saints, whose ordinary members happen to be not just he and his closest theological friends. In the Church there are *confessions*. Even in the Mennonite Church there is a confession called after the small Swiss village of Schleitheim ! Why should a free theologian not pay loving respect to these confessions as guidance in reading, explaining, and applying the Scriptures? True, he does not owe them the freedom of his thought and speech. He is not

bound by them. He will not listen to them very carefully. He will be free to express what they already have expressed, to express it better if he has the talent to do so. He is equally free to acknowledge their much better formulation of what he wants to say. He is free, therefore, to say in his own terms what they already have said.

In the Church there are *fathers* : father Luther, father Calvin, other fathers. Why should a free theologian not be their son and disciple? But why should he insist on complete agreement with them? Why should he artificially reinterpret their findings until Luther is in agreement with him and says what he himself so badly wants to say? Why should he not respect the freedom of the fathers and let them express their wisdom and then learn from them what in his own freedom he may and can learn from them?

In the Church there are also *church governments*. Here in Germany they are even embodied in bishops. These have power to speak their mighty word through pastoral letters within the framework of their own theology which may not always be infallible. They have also power to examine, perhaps even to institute or destitute, certainly to recommend or to withhold recommendation. Why should the free theologian not at least tolerate them as they, in their mildness and prudence, as a rule tolerate him? He will certainly not become their spokesman and subordinate. Nor will he disdain the acknowledgement that a leading church figure may think and say at times the theologically right thing. He really does not—or does he?— want to get a complex, to be misled into opposition against the leadership of the Church and to feed upon his hostility until it becomes the principle of his inter-

pretation of half, if not the whole, New Testament.
More is at stake than the pro and con of the confessions,
of Luther and Calvin, of the, alas, questionable church
government. All this is only a sectarian pro and con.
A free theologian is not a man of a sect. He thinks and
he speaks his definite " Yes " or " No." He is a man
of action, not of reaction. His freedom is not primarily
" freedom from " but " freedom for." He bewares of
becoming enmeshed in a friend-foe relationship. The
free theologian loves positive tasks. The Christian
community, its gathering, nurture, and mission in the
world, are at stake, and the free theologian knows this.
He does his research and teaching in and for the community, as one of its members entrusted with this
particular task and, hopefully, with the gift to carry it
through. Private Christianity is not Christianity at all.
Private theology is not free theology; it is not theology
at all.

(5) A free theologian works in *communication* with
other theologians. He grants them the enjoyment of
the same freedom with which he is entrusted. Maybe he
listens to them and reads their books with only subdued
joy, but at least he listens to them and reads them. He
knows that the selfsame problems with which he is
preoccupied may be seen and dealt with in a way
different from his own. Perhaps sincerity forbids him
from following or accompanying some of his fellow
theologians. Perhaps he is forced to oppose and sharply
contradict many, if not most, of his co-workers. He is
not afraid of the *rabies theologorum*. But he refuses to
part company with them, not only personally and intel-
lectually but, above all, spiritually, just as he does not
want to be dropped by them. He believes in the forgiveness of both his theological sins and theirs, if they

are found guilty of some. He will not pose as the detector and judge of their sins. Not yielding one iota where he cannot responsibly do so, he continues to consider the divine and human freedom in store for them. He waits for them and asks them to wait for him. Our sadly lacking yet indispensable theological co-operation depends directly or indirectly on whether or not we are willing to wait for one another, perhaps lamenting, yet smiling with tears in our eyes. Surely in such forbearance we could dispense with the hard, bitter, and contemptuous thoughts and statements about each other, with the bitter-sweet book reviews and the mischievous footnotes we throw at each other, and with whatever works of darkness there are! Is it clear in our minds that the concept of the " theological adversary " is profane and illegitimate? From my experience I would say that the Anglo-Saxon theologians, the fundamentalists probably notwithstanding, have a far better grasp of what I would like to call the " freedom of communication " than we Continentals do. They certainly do not all love each other overwhelmingly. But they treat each other as fellow creatures. We do not always act likewise. There is no ground for believing ourselves justified because of our, perhaps only illusionary, greater depth of thought.

These remarks need to be continued and drawn together systematically. Just think of the important issue of the existence and the reflection of the free theologian in his relationship to Roman Catholicism or to the prevailing political climate. Completeness, however, has not been my goal here. I merely wished to let a concrete example guide your reflection about the gift of freedom as the foundation of evangelical ethics. Therefore, I break off and close with a Biblical quotation in spite of what I said. It is an imperative, full of exegetical and other implications. Many of us are likely to have it interpreted and applied more than once with other people in mind. To-day we are asked to hear it for ourselves, as theologians, hopefully as free theologians : " Finally, brethren, whatever is true, whatever is honourable, whatever is just, whatever is pure, whatever is lovely, whatever is gracious, if there is any excellence, if there is anything worthy of praise, think about these things . . . and the peace of God will be with you."